Contents

of special interest...

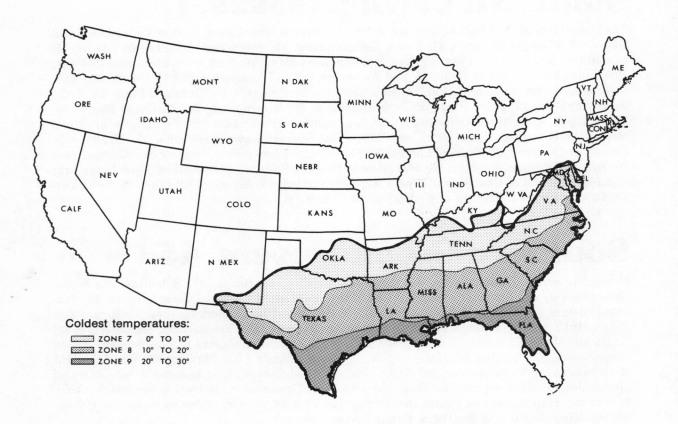

Coldest temperatures:

ZONE 7   0° TO 10°
ZONE 8   10° TO 20°
ZONE 9   20° TO 30°

Bold line delineates the area for which this book was written.

Southern Lawns and Groundcovers

Richard Duble
James Carroll Kell

Pacesetter Press
A Division of Gulf Publishing Company • Houston, Texas

Southern Lawns and Groundcovers

Library of Congress Catalog Card Number 77-73533
ISBN O-88415-426-2

Designed by Susan Corte
Edited by B.J. Lowe

Illustrated by
Terry J. Moore

1. Landscape Gardening.
2. Lawns. I. Title.

Southern Lawn Grasses

The concept of a manicured grass lawn can be traced back to the 13th century, when the English developed the lawn for bowling and cricket. But it wasn't until the 16th century that grass lawns became popular in England and Europe. When you consider that it wasn't until 1830 that an Englishman invented and patented the first mowing machine, the slow development of the grass lawn concept is more easily understood.

In the southern United States the use of pure grass stands for lawns was not widespread until the 20th century. Prior to that time a manicured grass lawn was a status symbol of the very wealthy: it was more common to find a vegetation-free surface for the front yard. The yard was swept or raked rather than mowed. It was not until the mass production of the lawn mower that interest in grass lawns increased in this country.

Much of the early knowledge of lawn culture evolved from practices originated in England. Lawn culture was an art attained through experience and trial-and-error, the secrets being passed from generation to generation. The secrets of lawn culture were kept within the family much as were the recipes for favorite dishes and beverages. It has only been during this century that turfgrass culture was based on scientific observation and research. Most of the advances in the science of turfgrass culture—improved grasses, speciality fertilizers, lawn pesticides and specialized equipment—have occurred since World War II.

Today, U.S. homeowners spend more than $10 billion annually on lawn maintenance. A 1975 survey in Florida estimated that $345 million was spent annually on individual home lawn

Lawns provide beauty . . .

And greetings . . .

And playgrounds . . .

And exercise.

maintenance in that state. Or, on an individual basis, the average homeowner in Florida spent $140 in 1974 on lawn maintenance. This estimate does not include any charges for labor on the part of the homeowner. A similar estimate for Texas projected a cost of $135 for lawn maintenance per homeowner.

How to Use this Section

The lawns section of this book has been written and designed for three levels of maintenance—intensive, moderate and low—so that you can give your lawn the maintenance you choose. Intensive-maintenance programs are designed to produce high-quality turf—uniform, dense, fine-textured, dark green color and pest-free with a high requirement for equipment, materials and labor. Moderate-maintenance programs are designed to produce an attractive lawn with only supplemental watering and fertilization; and low-maintenance programs are designed for no irrigation and only minimum fertilization. It's up to you to decide which program to follow depending on the time and money you have to spend.

Intensively maintained lawns will require an effective watering system (preferably an automatic system), mowing at 3 to 5-day intervals, monthly fertilization, annual dethatching and aeration, and a preventive pest control program for insects, diseases, and weeds. Such a program will cost approximately $50 to $60 per 1,000 square feet of lawn per year, not including labor.

A moderate lawn maintenance program will involve occasional watering, mowing on a 7- to 10-day schedule, spring and fall fertilization, and curative pest control. The cost of such a program will range from $20 to $40 per 1,000 square feet per year, depending on the grass variety. Centipede and Bahia grasses are the least expensive to maintain and St. Augustine, the most.

A low-maintenance program includes annual fall fertilization, and mowing at 14- to 21-day intervals. Carpet grass, Bahia grass, and centipede grass are good for such a program, and the cost should be less than $10 dollars per 1,000 square feet per year.

THE LAWN GRASSES

Over 5,000 species of grasses can be found throughout the world, yet fever than 25 species are adapted for turf use. The ability to tolerate close, frequent mowing and to produce a dense cover distinguishes a turfgrass from other grasses. In the South, only those turfgrasses that tolerate warm, humid conditions can be used successfully. Thus, of the 5,000 grass species, only about five are ideally suited for the South: St. Augustine grass, Bermuda grass, centipede grass, Bahia grass, and carpet grass. Other grasses can be grown in the South, but conditions here put them at a disadvantage. Zoysia grass can be grown only under intensive management; otherwise, Bermuda grass and weedy species which are better adapted to our hot, humid conditions will dominate zoysia. Tall fescue can be grown only in the northern-most portion of the South; but even there, plant diseases decimate tall fescue during the summer months.

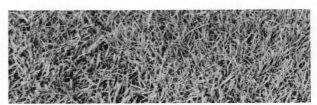

Bermuda grass

St. Augustine grass

Centipede grass

Carpet grass

Bahia grass

The five grasses ideally suited to the South

Grass as a Plant

The grass plant consists of stems, roots, leaves, and buds. The grass stem is made up of a series of nodes (swollen joints) and internodes (stem segments between nodes). The internode is hollow; the node is always solid. The stem may be upright as in tall fescues or decumbent as in St. Augustine grass; it may be simple as in tall fescue or freely branching as in Bermuda grass. Branches (lateral stems) arise only at the node in the axile of the leaf sheath. Some grasses have a stem that grows along the surface of the ground that produces roots and leaves at the nodes. Such stems are called *stolons* and the grasses that have them are called *stoloniferous*.

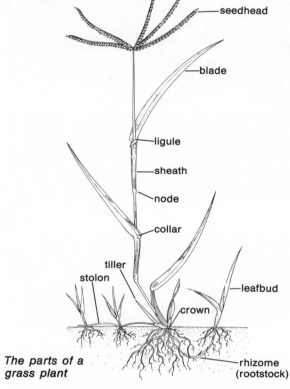

The parts of a grass plant

seedhead
blade
ligule
sheath
node
collar
tiller
stolon
leafbud
crown
rhizome (rootstock)

With the exception of tall fescue, all of the turfgrasses adapted to the South are stoloniferous grasses, or grasses with above-ground runners or stems. Thus, these grasses have a creeping-type growth habit that we have to combat with frequent edging or trimming of the walkways, gardens, and curbs they overrun. This is in contrast to the northern lawn grasses, which have an erect-type growth habit. A major advantage to lawn grasses with a creeping-type growth habit is their ability to establish or cover fast and to recover rapidly from injury. Grasses with erect growth habits, such as tall fescue, must be replanted when the lawn is damaged by insects, diseases or man.

The creeping growth habit of St. Augustine grass.

In some grasses, the stems grow underground and produce new plants at the nodes. Such stems are called *rhizomes* and the grasses are called *rhizomatous*. Bermuda grass and zoysia grass are examples of rhizomatous grasses.

The basic structural unit of the grass plant is the leaf. The grass leaf originates at the base of the node and consists of the leaf sheath which surrounds the stem and the leaf blade. Shoot buds arise at the node in the axile of the leaf sheath. Roots also arise at the node. Thus, the grass plant consists of a leaf blade, a leaf sheath, a stem segment with a bud, and a root system. The root system takes up water and nutrients; the leaf manufactures food (takes CO_2 from the air and water and minerals from the soil to produce carbohydrates, fats and protein); the stem stores the food; and growth occurs by the production of new shoots from the bud. These new shoots are referred to as *tillers*.

Turf density is determined by the number of new tillers produced—the more tillers produced, the greater the turf density. Tillering is common from spring through fall in warm season grasses and can be stimulated by mowing, fertilizing and watering. Cultural practices that restrict tillering include infrequent mowing, mowing too high, nitrogen deficiency and improper watering.

All grasses have fibrous root systems. In turfgrass species having an erect growth habit (non-creeping growth habit) roots originate from the basal nodes of the main shoot and from tillers near the ground level. Roots also develop from the nodes of stolons and rhizomes of grasses with a creeping-type growth habit. Root growth begins in early spring and continues throughout the growing season. Adequate soil moisture, aeration and fertilization are essential to the development of a deep, extensive root system which, in turn, is required to produce a healthy, vigorous lawn. Cultural practices that restrict root growth include frequent mowing at a very low height, excessive nitrogen fertilization during the growing season, phosphorus or potassium deficiencies, excess thatch accumulation or overwatering.

Kinds of Grasses

Turfgrasses differ in appearance as well as in adaptation to specific environmental conditions and cultural requirements. The most important decision you make about your lawn is the grass species or variety you plant. Selecting the right grass for a particular lawn simplifies the entire lawn maintenance program.

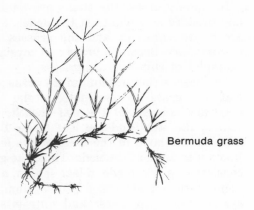

Bermuda grass

withstanding heavy use. The Bermuda grasses lack shade tolerance, which limits their use in many lawn situations. They are also considered high-maintenance grasses since they require frequent mowing, annual fertilization, and occasional watering.

Pest problems include white grub, scale insects, Bermuda grass mites, sod webworms, cutworms, and armyworms. Dollar spot and leaf spot diseases are also a problem on Bermuda grasses.

Bermuda grasses are warm-season perennials adapted to a wide range of soil temperatures and cultural conditions. Bermuda grass provides a very quick cover.

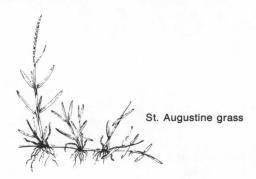

St. Augustine grass

Bermuda grass. Bermuda grasses are warm-season perennial grasses adapted to a wide range of temperatures, soils, and management conditions. They green-up in early spring and continue growing until the first killing frost in the fall. The Bermuda grasses remain dormant (brown) as long as soil temperatures are below 60°F. Common Bermuda grass is the only variety that can be established from seed. All other varieties of Bermuda grass must be established by vegetative methods. All of the Bermuda grasses spread by both stolons and rhizomes; thus, they cover rapidly. They are deep-rooted grasses and root readily at the nodes, forming a very dense, strong sod capable of

St. Augustine Grass. St. Augustine grass is also a warm-season perennial species adapted to the Gulf Coast area. Poor cold tolerance restricts the northern boundary of St. Augustine grass. This grass is currently propagated entirely by vegetative methods, although some growers are beginning to investigate commercial seed production of the grass.

St. Augustine is a coarse-textured grass that spreads by above-ground runners, or stolons. The stolons are much larger in diameter than those of Bermuda grass, and the leaves are much wider. In contrast to Bermuda grass, St. Augustine does not produce rhizomes and, consequently, is less

Bermuda Grass Varieties

Variety	Description	Mowing height & frequency	Nitrogen (lbs/1,000 sq. ft.)	Problems
Common	Medium texture; responds well to management; widely used for lawns	1-2 inches, 7-10 days	2-3	Bermuda grass mites, white grub, leaf spot diseases
Tifgreen	Fine texture; light green; forms very dense turf; abundant seedheads	1 inch or less, 5 days	4-6	Bermuda grass mite, white grub, leaf spot diseases, dollar spot and brownpatch
Tifdwarf	Fine texture; low-growing; dark green; very dense turf; abundant seedheads	½ inch or less, 3-5 days	4-6	Bermuda grass mites, white grub, leaf spot diseases, dollar spot and brownpatch, has tendency to accumulate thatch
Tiflawn	Medium texture; dark green; vigorous	1-2 inches, 7 days	3-4	Bermuda grass mites, white grub, leaf spot diseases
Tifway	Fine texture; dark green; vigorous; very dense; produces very few seedheads	1 inch 5-7 days	3-4	resistant to Bermuda grass mites; otherwise same as Tifdwarf
Ormond	Medium texture; dark green; good low-temperature color retention; used mostly in Florida for lawns	1 inch, 5-7 days	3-4	Same as Tifgreen

St. Augustine Varieties

Variety	Description	Mowing height & frequency	Nitrogen (lbs/1,000 sq. ft.)	Problems
Common	Medium texture; light green; vigorous, dense turf	1-2 inches, 7-10 days	2-3 lbs.	Chinch bugs, white grub, brownpatch, leaf spot and SAD
Floratine	Medium texture; blue-green; low-growing	1-2 inches, 7-10 days	2-3 lbs.	Chinch bugs, white grub, brownpatch, leaf spot and SAD
Bitter Blue	Medium texture; blue-green; dense turf	1-2 inches, 7-10 days	2-3 lbs.	Chinch bugs, white grub, brownpatch, leaf spot and SAD
Floratam	Coarse texture; blue-green; vigorous	2 inches, 7-10 days	3-4 lbs.	White grub, brownpatch, leaf spot, poor cold tolerance, poor shade tolerance

troublesome to remove from flower beds and gardens. But it does require frequent edging along walks and curbs. St. Augustine is the most shade-tolerant of the warm-season turfgrasses. Although St. Augustine loses color and becomes dormant during cold winter months, it retains its color at temperatures as much as 10° below that which discolors Bermuda grass. Were it not for the insect and disease problems of St. Ausustine grass, it would be the ideal turfgrass. It produces a dense, weed-free turf with little fertilization. St. Augustine is not as drought-tolerant as Bermuda grass and requires supplemental watering during summer months to maintain color and growth.

Pest problems include chinch bugs, white grub, brownpatch, leaf spot and St. Augustine Decline (SAD). One variety of St. Augustine, Floratam, is resistant to SAD and chinch bugs. However, it is less cold and shade-tolerant than other St. Augustine varieties. Floratine and Bitter Blue varieties are produced primarily in Florida; Floratam is available throughout the lower South.

Floratam, a St. Augustine variety, is resistant to St. Augustine Decline (SAD) as well as chinch bugs, though it is less cold- and shade-tolerant than other St. Augustine varieties.

Bahia grass

Bahia Grass. Bahia was introduced into the U.S. from South America in 1913. It is widely used for lawns in Florida and is adapted to sandy soils all along the Gulf Coast. Bahia does not spread as fast as St. Augustine or Bermuda grass. It has thick, short rhizomes and rather broad leaves. Yet, with close mowing it produces a dense turf. Bahia has a deep, extensive root system and is quite drought-tolerant. A characteristic of Bahia that limits its use as a lawn grass is its prolific seedhead production. Several days after mowing, a new crop of seedstalks develops. The seedstalks may reach a height of 1 to 2 feet.

Bahia Grass Varieties

Varieties	Description	Mowing height & frequency	Problems
Common	Short, broad leaves, somewhat hairy; light green; seedstalks 12 to 18 inches tall; forms an open coarse turf	1-2 inches, 10-14 days	Poor cold tolerance
Pensacola	Long, narrow leaves, light green; deep root system; seedstalks 24 to 36 inches tall; good cold tolerance	1-2 inches, 7-10 days	Abundant seedstalks; sensitive to iron chlorosis
Argentine	Long, broad leaves, dark green; seedstalks 18 to 24 inches tall; forms dense turf	1-2 inches, 7-10 days	Abundant seedstalks
Paraguay	Short, narrow, hairy leaves; leaves have a grayish appearance; seedstalks 12 to 18 inches tall	1-2 inches, 10-14 days	Poor cold tolerance
Wilmington	Narrow leaves; dark green; good cold tolerance; seedstalks few and shorter than other varieties	1-2 inches, 10-14 days	Highly susceptible to dollar spot

Centipede Grass Varieties

Variety	Description	Mowing height & frequency	Nitrogen (lbs/1,000 sq. ft.)	Problems
Common	Medium texture; light green; spreads by stolons; forms dense sod; does well in partial shade	1-2 inches, 10-14 days	1-2	Winterkills below 15°F; centipede decline
Oaklawn	Same as common except bluish-green color; more cold-tolerant	1-2 inches, 10-14 days	1-2	Winterkills below 10°F, centipede decline

Bahia grass has been used extensively for stabilizing road shoulders along highways throughout the Southeast. It is satisfactory where low maintenance is desired and quality is not important. Bahia grasses can be established from either seed or sod, and several varieties are available for lawn use.

Pest problems of Bahia include white grub, armyworms, dollarspot and leaf spot, but the prolific production of seedstalks is more of a nuisance than the pests.

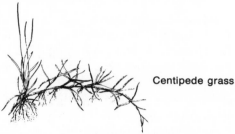

Centipede grass

Centipede Grass. Centipede grass was introduced in the U.S. in 1919 from Southeastern Asia. It is often called a "lazy man's grass" because of its low maintenance requirements. Centipede is a low-growing, stoloniferous, perennial grass with a slightly finer texture than St. Augustine grass. It tolerates partial shade and is not as salt-tolerant as St. Ausustine. Slightly to moderately acid soils are favorable for growing centipede (pH 6.0-7.0). It is a relatively shallow-rooted turfgrass and so is not as drought-tolerant as St. Augustine, Bermuda or Bahia grasses. It is among the first of the grasses to turn brown during continuous dry conditions.

Centipede lawns should not be fertilized more than once a year. Excessive use of fertilizer has been implicated as a contributing factor to centipede decline—a condition where the grass does not recover in the spring or where it begins to grow briefly and then dies. The specific cause of centipede decline has not been identified, but the incidence of the problem increases with the use of nitrogen fertilizers.

Centipede grass is another turfgrass that can be established from either seed, sprigs or sod. A complete lawncover can be developed faster from seed than from sprigs. Although the seed is expensive, a pound of seed will plant 2,000 to 4,000 square feet of lawn area. If you want an improved selection of centipede grass, such as Oaklawn, it must be planted from vegetative material.

Other than centipede decline, the grass is relatively free of problems. Iron chlorosis is more of a problem than insects or diseases. White grub, ground pearls, and brownpatch are the major pest problems of centipede grass.

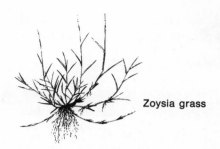

Zoysia grass

Zoysia Grass. Zoysia grasses are excellent for turf when they are planted and managed properly. A good zoysia lawn is attractive and wear-resistant, is not invaded by weeds and other grasses during the growing season, and is subject to little damage from insects and diseases. However, rust, a fungus disease, can severely discolor zoysia lawns in the fall. Zoysia will form a dense turf in partial shade but will thin out in dense shade. It is less drought-tolerant than Bermuda grass. Zoysia is slower-growing than Bahia, Bermuda or St. Augustine grasses and requires much longer to establish a complete cover. However, it should be mowed nearly as often as a Bermuda grass lawn if a uniform, attractive appearance is desired. Otherwise, it develops a puffy, spongy turf that becomes very difficult to mow. Because of its slow growth, it is not as much of a pest as Bermuda grass in flower beds and gardens.

The Zoysia grasses may be established from seed, sprigs or sod. A clean seedbed is necessary for the most rapid establishment of a zoysia cover. Competition from other grasses may mean that 3 or more years will be required to obtain a complete zoysia turf. Sod plugs 2 inches in diameter planted on 12-inch centers may take 2 years to provide the cover that Bermuda grass or St. Augustine would give in 3 months. Zoysia sprigged in a clean seedbed at the rate of 10 bushels per 1,000 square feet should give a cover in one growing season with good growing conditions, if other grasses and weeds are kept out.

Zoysia japonica, often called Japanese lawn grass, was introduced into the United States from North Korea in 1930. *Zoysia japonica* is a coarse textured grass that produces a poor-quality lawn. It is very cold-tolerant and can be established from seed.

Manila grass *(Zoysia matrella)* was introduced from Manila in 1911. It is finer textured than Japanese lawn grass, but less cold-tolerant. It is dark green in color, very wear-resistant and makes a beautiful lawn.

Meyer zoysia is an improved strain of *Zoysia japonica.* When Meyer zoysia was first released in

Variety	Description	Mowing height & frequency	Nitrogen (lbs/1,000 sq. ft.)	Problems
Japanese lawn grass	Coarse texture; good cold tolerance; may be seeded	2 inches, 7-10 days	2-3 lbs.	Poor quality
Manilagrass	Medium texture; dark green; may be seeded; less cold tolerant than Japanese lawn grass	2 inches, 7-10 days	2-3 lbs.	Slow to establish from seed or sprigs
Meyer	Medium texture; dark green; develops a dense turf, must be sprigged or sodded	1-2 inches, 7-10 days	2-3 lbs.	Slow to establish; tends to develop a thatch; difficult to mow
Emerald	Fine texture; dark green; develops a very dense, compact turf; must be sprigged or sodded	1-2 inches, 7-10 days	2-3 lbs.	Slow to establish; develops a thatch; difficult to mow

1951, it sold for approximately $45 a square yard (today it's $3.00 a square yard). Meyer grows much more rapidly than Manila grass and has a dark green color with a texture between that of Manila grass and Japanese lawn grass. Meyer zoysia is well adapted to the transition zone (between zone 6 and 7), where it is too cold for most southern grasses and too hot and humid for bluegrass. It produces a dense turf that is resistant to weed invasion. Like other zoysia grasses, it turns brown after the first frost and remains dormant until spring. Meyer must be planted from vegetative material.

Emerald zoysia is a hybrid zoysia that produces a dark green, very dense turf. It tolerates drought, partial shade, has good winter hardiness, and is among the finest lawn grasses.

White grub, brownpatch, and rust are the chief pest problems of the zoysia grasses, but their main limitation as southern lawn grass is their slow rate of establishment. This gives common Bermuda grass a competitive advantage, making it a serious weed problem in zoysia lawns.

Carpet grass

Carpet Grass. Carpet grass is a coarse-textured perennial species that spreads by above-ground runners, or stolons. Carpet grass is often confused with St. Augustine, but they are two distinct grasses. In contrast to St. Augustine, the stolons of carpet grass are small, the leaf tips are blunt, and the seedstalks are long and slender. Carpetgrass generally is a lighter green color, does not produce as dense a turf, and is not as shade-tolerant as St. Augustine.

Carpet grass, a good low-maintenance lawn grass, is a lighter green than St. Augustine grass and does not produce as dense a turf.

Carpet grass is less winter hardy than centipede or Bermuda grass and should be confined to the lower South. It is less drought-tolerant than St. Augustine and is best adapted to muck soils or sandy soils where moisture is near the surface. Carpet grass is only recommended for low-maintenance lawns where quality is not the objective. Perhaps the most objectionable feature of carpet grass is the numerous tall seedstalks produced throughout the summer. Because of this habit, carpet grass lawns should be mowed at 10- to 14-day intervals at a height of 2 inches. You'll need a rotary mower to remove the unsightly seedstalks.

Carpet grass is a native of the West Indies and was introduced into the United States in the early

1800s. It spread throughout the moist soils of the coastal plains from Texas to North Carolina. It is propagated from seed produced commercially in Louisiana. A fast cover of carpet grass can be produced by seeding at a rate of 1-2 pounds per 1,000 square feet; large areas can be effectively established by planting at a rate of ½ pound per 1,000 square feet. Carpet grass should be planted in early spring. The seedbed should be kept moist until the grass is established.

Carpet grass performs well on moderately acid soils with low fertility. (If carpet grass is fertilized too often, Bermuda grass will crowd it out.) In most cases lime is not required, but applying a complete fertilizer at planting time will hasten the rate of cover. Carpet grass will not tolerate dry soil conditions for a long period. On deep, sandy soils it will need watering during dry periods. No improved varieties of carpet grass are available.

Carpet grass has few pest problems because of its low maintenance level; white grub, brownpatch, and leaf spots will attack it, but they are seldom serious problems.

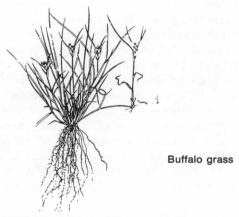

Buffalo grass

Buffalo Grass. Buffalo grass is a fine-textured, low-growing perennial grass native to South Central Texas and areas west and north of there. It should not be planted as a lawn grass in the southeastern states. Buffalo grass is very drought-tolerant and will survive the dry conditions of West Texas without supplemental watering. However, it turns straw colored during dry periods. Buffalo spreads by surface runners only and is easily controlled in flower beds and gardens.

Buffalo grass is not shade-tolerant. It thrives on fertile, well-aerated, clay soils and can be established from seed or sod. Seed should be treated to increase germination and planted at a rate of 2 to 3 pounds per 1,000 square feet. New plantings should be fertilized with a complete fertilizer at a rate equivalent to 1 pound of nitrogen per 1,000 square feet. Excessive water and fertilizer will promote

Bermuda grass and weeds that crowd out buffalo grass.

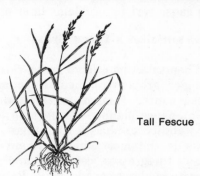

Tall Fescue

Tall Fescue. Tall fescue is a cool season, perennial bunch grass. It is a coarse-textured grass that forms a weak sod. Tall fescue tolerates moderate shade and is quite drought-tolerant. It is best adapted to the "transitional zone" of the U.S., which includes the northern portion of the South. In this area tall fescue will remain green all year with supplemental watering during the summer.

Tall fescue should be planted in early fall at a rate of 6 to 8 pounds of seed per 1,000 square feet. In the South, spring plantings of tall fescue often require replanting the following fall. New plantings should be fertilized with a complete fertilizer at a rate of 1 pound of nitrogen per 1,000 square feet. Fertilize at the same rate again in early spring and early summer; do *not* fertilize tall fescue during the hot summer months.

Tall fescue should be mowed at weekly intervals, at a height of 2 to 3 inches. The greater height should be used under shaded conditions and during the summer.

Proper watering is important to the survival of tall fescue. Water should be applied to wet the soil at least 4 inches deep. Don't water again until the grass shows moisture stress (wilted condition, curled leaves, grayish color). Tall fescue requires about the same amount of supplemental water as St. Augustine grass.

Several varieties of tall fescue are available, but Kentucky 31 tall fescue has performed as well as newer varieties in tests throughout the South.

White grub, fusarium blight, brownpatch, and leaf spot are the major pests with this lawn grass.

Establishing a New Lawn

Give careful consideration to selection of the proper grass, soil preparation, planting method and care during the establishment period.

Mistakes in planning and preparation at this stage can cause serious problems later on.

How to Select a Lawn Grass

When selecting a lawn grass, things you should consider are environmental factors (shade, soil type, winter temperatures) and the level of maintenance planned. Turfgrasses differ in their adaptability to shaded conditions: St. Augustine grass is the most shade-tolerant of the warm season turfgrasses; centipede and zoysia grasses tolerate moderate shade, while Bahia will tolerate only limited shade. The Bermuda grasses require full sunlight for best performance. In the northern parts of the South where tall fescue is adapted (zones 6 and 7), it may be used for shaded lawns. Thus, if shade is a factor, the selection of a grass variety is a critical decision.

Soil type will largely determine the performance of the turfgrasses: centipede and Bahia are best adapted to deep sandy soils such as those found in Florida and along the Gulf Coast (also, centipede should not be used in soils where the pH is 7.5 or higher); carpet grass, tall fescue, and Bahia tolerate poorly drained soils, whereas St. Augustine, centipede, zoysia and Bermuda prefer well drained sites. St. Augustine and Bermuda grass will survive salty soil conditions; but centipede and Bahia will not. If you don't know the salinity or pH of your soil, you can send a soil sample through your county agricultural Extension agent to soil testing laboratories to obtain information on soil characteristics.

Temperature extremes also limit the adaptability of some grasses. Tall fescue and zoysia are

St. Augustine grass is the most shade-tolerant of the warm-season grasses.

the most tolerant to low temperatures; Bermuda, St. Augustine, centipede and Bahia grasses are less cold hardy and may be killed at temperatures below 10°F. As discussed in the section on grass varieties, some varieties within a species tolerate much lower temperatures than other varieties. For example, Ormond Bermuda grass is rather tolerant to low winter temperatures, but Tifgreen or Tifdwarf Bermuda might winterkill. Floratam St. Augustine is also highly susceptible to cold temperatures and must be restricted to the southern boundaries of the Gulf Coast area.

The cultural requirements of turfgrasses are another important consideration in selecting a lawn grass. For example, the hybrid Bermuda grasses require frequent mowing, high fertiliza-

Factors to Consider When Selecting a Lawn Grass

	Site Description							
Level of maintenance	Full sunlight	Partial shade	Heavy shade	Poorly drained soil	Low soil pH (below 6)	High soil pH (above 7.5)	Low winter temp. (below 10°)	Saline soils
Intensive	1,2,4,7,9	1,2,7,9	1,2,9	9	4,7,9	1,2,4,7,9	7,9	1,2,4
Moderate	1,2,3,5,6,7,9	1,2,5,6,7,9	1,2,9	5,9	5,6	1,2,3,5,7,9	7,9	1,2,3
Low	5,6,8,9,10	5,6,8,9	6,8,9	5,8,9	5,6,8,9	5,9,10	9,10	8

1-St. Augustine grass (common)
2-St. Augustine grass (Floratam)
3-Common Bermuda grass
4-Hybrid Bermuda grass
5-Bahia grass
6-Centipede grass
7-Zoysia grass
8-Carpet grass
9-Tall fescue (northern-most areas only)
10-Buffalo grass (southwest only)

tion rates, and frequent watering—they should be used only under intensive lawn care situations. On the other hand, Bahia and carpet grass are low-maintenance turfgrasses and should not be used where intensive cultural practices are to be employed. St. Augustine is intermediate in terms of cultural requirements and is best adapted to moderate lawn care programs. The chart on page 10 will help you select a grass for your situation.

Seedbed Preparation

Your only opportunity to modify soil conditions and provide a good seedbed for your turfgrass is prior to grass establishment. Although selecting a grass variety adapted to local soil conditions is the most reasonable approach, soils can be modified to meet requirements of grasses otherwise unadapted to your area. For example, a poorly drained site which is normally suitable only for Bahia, carpet grass or tall fescue might be modified to improve drainage and provide an adequate environment for the growth of St. Augustine, Bermuda grass or other more desirable lawn grasses.

The addition of organic material is another way to modify your soil. Organic matter can improve the moisture and nutrient content of your soil as well as its physical conditions (friability, porosity, permeability, etc.). Peat moss is the ideal organic amendment, but it is impractical. Composted rice hulls, pine bark, sawdust or gin trash are suitable and reasonably priced organic materials. A minimum of 10 cubic yards of organic material per 1,000 square feet is adequate. The organic amendment should be incorporated or mixed with the top 2 to 4 inches of soil. In sandy or light soils this can be accomplished with a hand-operated rototiller. In heavy clay soils, tractor-powered equipment will be required to incorporate this material effectively.

Acid soils (pH below 6.5) can be modified by the addition of limestone at a rate of 25-50 pounds per 1,000 square feet. The limestone, like the organic material, should be incorporated or mixed with the top 2 to 4 inches of soil. Soils with a very high pH (8.5 or higher) or tight clay soils can be improved by the incorporation of gypsum at a rate of 50-100 pounds per 1,000 square feet. Some soils can be improved by adding phosphorus and other fertilizer nutrients in the seedbed prior to grass establishment. Again, information on the nutrient status of your soil can be obtained through local agricultural Extension offices or through soil test results.

The final steps in preparing your seedbed for grass establishment include removing rocks and other debris, final grading, smoothing and firming. Since it is difficult to alter the contour of the lawn after grass establishment, be sure that grades are properly established and that the surface is smoothed prior to planting. Tractor-mounted blades or scrapers are required for the rough grading and smoothing, but some hand work may be required to smooth the final grade. If the soil is loose, drag a heavy carpet or doormat across the area to smooth the surface and fill small depressions. In the construction of a new home, contractors often bury building materials and debris such as bricks, builders sand, plastic, wood and other materials rather than going to the expense of hauling them off. Avoid this problem and remove debris prior to establishing grass.

Since it is difficult to alter the contour of your lawn after grass has established, be sure that grades are properly established and that the surface is smooth prior to planting. Tractor-mounted blades with scrapers are required for the rough grading and smoothing, but some handwork may be necessary.

PLANTING METHODS

Depending on grass varieties, lawns may be seeded, sprigged or solid sodded. Seeding is the easiest and cheapest method of planting and solid sodding is the most expensive. But there are advantages and disadvantages to each method of planting a new lawn.

Seeding

Since grass seed is very small and less vigorous than that of larger-seeded plants, seedbed preparation, planting method, and post-planting care are very important. The seedbed should be smooth, firm, and moist at the time of planting.

Purchase high-quality lawn seed: factors such as germination percent and purity are shown on the labels of all containers of commercial lawn seed.

Certain minimum germination and purity percentages should be tolerated when buying lawn seed. Seed whose germination percentage is lower than the suggested minimum (see the table below) should cost less per pound and require a higher seeding rate. Likewise, as the percent purity decreases, the price should decrease and seeding rate should increase.

Seeding rates are also critical in terms of the time required to establish the lawn and the overall cost of seeding a lawn. Generally, the higher the seeding rate, the faster the cover; where very low seeding rates are used, the time required to develop a cover is usually prohibitive. But with too high a seeding rate, the cost of establishment is generally prohibitive and the time for the development of a healthy turf may also be delayed since the seedlings compete with one another for moisture and nutrients.

Ideally, grass seed should be planted at a depth of ¼ to ½ inch, but special equipment is required to achieve this planting depth. Hand raking the yard followed by dragging or rolling may simulate those planting depths. Surface planting of grass seed can be successful, but moisture control is critical and difficult to achieve with this method. Frequent sprinkling or mulching is required if you plant the seed on the surface. Grass seed may be distributed by hand or by a drop-type or cyclone-type seeder. When planting very small-seeded grasses, such as Bermuda grass or centipede, the seed should be mixed with sand prior to planting for more uniform distribution. The amount of seed required per 1,000 square feet should be mixed with about a gallon of sand and spread uniformly over the 1,000-square foot area. The seed required

Distribute grass seed in two directions at right angles to one another to provide uniform coverage.

for a given area should be split into two lots and applied in two directions at right angles to one another.

Planting dates are also important for the successful establishment of a new lawn. The warm-

Suggested Minimums for Seed Germination and Purity of Lawn Seed

Grass species	Minimum germination (%)	Minimum purity (%)	Seeding rate (lbs/1,000 sq. ft.)
Bahia grass	70	80	4-6
Bermuda grass (common)	80	95	1-2
Buffalo grass	80	70	2-3
Carpet grass	70	80	2-3
Centipede grass	50	70	¼-½
St. Augustine grass*	70	80	¼-½
Tall fescue	90	95	6-8
Zoysia grass	50	95	1-2

*St. Augustine seed is not widely available.

season grasses (all those mentioned thus far, except tall fescue) should be planted in early spring to early summer and may be planted again in early fall. Mid-summmer and late fall or winter plantings should be avoided. Tall fescue should only be planted during the early fall months. Plantings made out of season often fail because of dry conditions or temperature extremes.

After a lawn is seeded, firm the soil and keep it moist until the grass is well established. Bermuda grass generally requires 7 to 10 days to germinate, whereas Bahia and centipede grass require 2 to 3 weeks. After the seed germinates, water every 2 or 3 days to maintain growth. Fertilize the lawn prior to seeding or after the grass has established, usually 3 to 4 weeks after planting. Apply a low analysis fertilizer such as 6-12-12 or 8-8-8 at a rate of 10 to 15 pounds per 1,000 square feet.

After seeding the lawn, firm the soil and keep it moist until the grass is well established.

Sprigging

The hybrid Bermuda grasses, St. Augustine and zoysia grasses are established by sprigging. A sprig is a small segment of either a stolon or a rhizome, with at least two nodes. Sprigs may be planted similar to grass seed, that is, they may be planted on the surface or they may be covered with about ¼ inch of soil. If sprigs are planted in rows, the rows should be 6 inches apart, with the sprigs 2 to 3 inches apart in the row. Recommended planting dates, watering, and fertilizing are the same for sprigging as for seeding.

Another method of planting lawns with either seed or sprigs is hydromulching. Hydro-mulching involves the application of a slurry of seed or sprigs and a fibrous mulch material to the surface of the lawn through a high-pressure applicator. The mulch along with the planting material is agitated in a tank with water and applied through a nozzle under pressure. The mulch is generally applied at a rate of 50 pounds per 1,000 square feet along with the recommended rate of planting material. Fertilizer may also be added along with the other materials. The mulch helps to hold moisture near the soil surface and provides a more favorable environment for germination of seed or sprigs. Mulched areas won't need watering as frequently as unmulched areas. Care should be taken to see that mulched sites are not over-watered. Hydro-mulching requires highly specialized equipment and must be done through the services of a professional landscape contractor.

Hydro-mulching is a good way to get a lawn going. The mulch helps hold moisture near the soil surface and provides a favorable environment for seed germination or sprig growth.

Rolling and smoothing a newly sprigged lawn.

Another method of sprigging involves the planting of 2- to 4-inch plugs of grass at 1- to 2-foot spacings. The plugs can be obtained by cutting a section of sod into small segments with a spade or knife. A square foot of sod can be divided into 10 to 30 plugs, depending on the size of the plugs. This planting method is relatively slow and requires a large amount of hand labor. An advantage is that watering is not as critical since the sprigs are already rooted and the roots are protected with soil. Another advantage is that grass can be planted out of season with a greater chance for success, again because the sprigs are already rooted and the roots are protected by soil. One disadvantage, other than the high amount of hand labor required, is that an uneven surface results unless you're very careful to plant the sod plugs at a uniform depth.

Square Feet of Sod Required to Plant 1,000 sq. ft. of Lawn

Plug Size (sq. inches)	If you space plugs at:			
	½'	1'	2'	3'
	You'll need (sq. ft.):			
2	110	28	7	3
3	250	62	16	7
4	440	111	28	12

Zoysia sod plugs, planted at 6-inch spacings, will cover an area in one year.

Solid Sodding

You can have an instant lawn by planting sod blocks end to end uniformly over a smooth, well-prepared bed. The bed should be prepared prior to delivery of the sod, and, at the time of planting, should be moist but not wet. Laying the sod blocks along a straight edge such as a curb or walk will help to keep them aligned. The edges of the sod blocks should contact one another without overlapping. Lay sod blocks in a staggered or checkerboard pattern. Immediately after sodding the lawn, water it. Don't let the lawn dry out until the sod has rooted into the bed (usually 7 to 10 days). In terms of initial costs for planting material, solid sodding with sod blocks is the most expensive method of planting. However, the advantages are

many: On sloping areas, you don't need to be concerned with erosion of topsoil if an area is solid sodded. Likewise, the homeowner does not need to be concerned with blowing dust, mud or weeds in a newly sodded lawn. Other methods of planting require 6-8 weeks in order to have a complete lawn cover; whereas, a solid sodded lawn provides an instant turf. A solid sodded lawn rarely requires replanting, whereas, a sprigged or seeded lawn frequently does. Thus, much of the savings anticipated by sprigging or seeding a lawn may be lost through the cost of replanting. For relatively small lawns—those 5,000 square feet or less—solid sodding may be the most practical method of planting.

When solid-sodding a lawn, lay the sod blocks in a staggered or checkerboard pattern.

Post Planting Care

The care that a new lawn receives for the first 6 to 8 months after planting largely determines its success or failure. Newly planted lawns should be fertilized at 3- to 4-week intervals until the lawn is completely covered. In the absence of soil test recommendations, a balanced, complete fertilizer such as a 12-12-12 or 8-8-8 should be applied at a rate equivalent to 1 pound of nitrogen per 1,000 square feet. Initially, water should be applied lightly and frequently to maintain a moist surface. Once the grass is established (usually 2 to 3 weeks after planting), water less frequently. At this point, water should be applied so that the soil is wet to a depth of 4 to 6 inches. Under such conditions, the lawn may go 3 to 4 days without irrigation. During the establishment period it is important not to allow the grass to suffer severe drought stress, which could delay coverage by several weeks.

Newly planted lawns should be mowed when the grass gets approximately 2 inches high. Mow back to a height of 1½ inches. (Bermuda grass should be mowed to 1 inch.) Close mowing during the estab-

lishment period stimulates tillering and increases the coverage rate of warm season grasses. After the initial mowing, newly planted lawns should be mowed weekly.

Herbicides to control weeds may be applied after the grass is well established, usually 3 to 4 weeks after planting. A heavy infestation of weeds could delay grass coverage by several months. For recommendations on specific herbicides, see pages 45-50. Ordinarily, mowing at the proper height and frequency and proper fertilization will eliminate or reduce weed problems.

Lawn Maintenance

Lawn care involves mowing, watering, fertilizing, accurate identification of problems, and the application of recommended pesticides. The time and effort you'll need to devote to your lawn will depend on the grass variety you select.

Intensively Maintained Lawns

Intensively maintained lawns should be restricted to the hybrid Bermuda grasses, zoysia grasses, and St. Augustine grass. You would want an intensively maintained lawn in an area with a high degree of visibility, such as around patio areas and pools, entrance ways, or surrounding decorative ornamental plantings and flower beds.

Intensively maintained lawns require some type of irrigation system, ideally, a completely automatic system which operates with a timer. Such a system provides a uniform, accurate, and timely application of water. If an automatic watering system is impractical, a quick-couple system with pemanently installed underground pipe can be used. Whatever system you use, give careful consideration to its design and installation: poorly designed and installed systems will produce continuous problems.

Intensively maintained lawns should receive about 1 inch of water per week throughout the growing season. Depending on the soil type, this amount of water should be applied in two or three applications. Sandy soils require frequent irrigation; heavier clay soils require less frequent watering. The uniformity of application of water is just as important as the amount of water applied. This can be determined easily by spreading cans or buckets around the lawn. Place some containers near the sprinkler head, others at intervals

between sprinkler heads, and still others at the outer edges of the irrigated area. After the cans are in place, turn on the system for 15-20 minutes. Then measure and record the depth of water in each container to determine the uniformity of application. If the depth of the water is approximately the same in each, the system is applying water uniformly. If the difference in the depth of water in the various containers is greater than 25%, corrective steps should be taken. Sprinkler head sizes, nozzle sizes, operating pressures, and spacing between heads may be adjusted to correct non-uniform water distribution. In addition, operating times for the various heads or various sections of the lawn may be adjusted to improve the uniformity of application of water. If you install a completely automatic system, adjust the timer so that the watering system operates in the early morning hours. Late afternoon and early evening watering is usually most convenient and is satisfactory for manual watering.

The mowing schedule for an intensively maintained lawn depends almost entirely on the grass variety. The hybrid Bermuda grasses require mowing at 3- to 5- day intervals, whereas St. Augustine or zoysia grass may be mowed at 5- to 7-day intervals. Mowing height also affects mowing intervals.

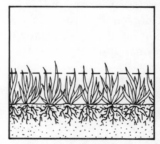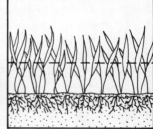

Mowing height depends on mowing frequency. Frequent mowings at low heights result in the best turf.

Generally, the shorter the grass is mowed, the more frequently it requires mowing. A hybrid Bermuda lawn mowed at a height of ½ inch will require mowing at 3-day intervals, whereas a lawn mowed at a height of 1 inch will require mowing at 5-day intervals. Likewise, St. Augustine grass mowed at a height of 1 inch will require mowing every 5 days; the same lawn mowed at a height of 2 inches may go 7 to 10 days between mowings.

If you mow at a height of 1 inch or less, use a reel-type mower rather than a rotary mower. The reel-type actually cuts the leaf blade, where the rotary mower simply tears the blade. Consequently, lawns mowed by a reel-type mower will have a much neater appearance than those mowed

If you mow at a height of 1 inch or less, use a reel-type mower (above) rather than a rotary mower. Reel-type mowers give the lawn a much neater appearance (they're necessary for hybrid Bermuda lawns).

with a rotary mower. Grass clippings should be collected and removed from intensively managed lawns, otherwise thatch accumulates rapidly. Intensively managed lawns should be scalped (to reduce thatch) in the early spring, about the time the grass begins to break dormancy. You can do this by lowering the mowing height ½ inch, mowing the lawn in two directions, and removing the grass clippings.

If you manage your lawn intensively, collect and remove grass clippings with each mowing; otherwise, thatch will accumulate rapidly.

Occasionally, perhaps every 2 or 3 years, intensively managed lawns require dethatching, or vertical mowing, to reduce thatch accumulation. Small lawns may be dethatched by hand with a dethatching rake. Larger areas will require a power vertical mower or dethatcher. This procedure thins the turf and pulls the dead tissue

to the surface where it can be collected and removed. Where thatch accumulations exceed ½ inch, it can create problems with mowing, watering, fertilizing, and pest control. Intensively managed lawns may also require occasional aeration to reduce surface compaction and to improve water penetration. To aerate the lawn, use a hollow spoon aerator that extracts soil cores. Solid spike aerators actually add to the compaction problem and so should be avoided.

Small lawns can be dethatched with a dethatching rake.

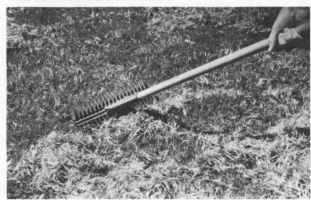

Larger lawns require a power vertical mower or dethatcher to reduce thatch.

Fertilization of intensively managed lawns should be based on soil test recommendations. Each year, collect a soil sample and send it to a soil testing laboratory through your local Extension office or a commercial laboratory. Intensively managed hybrid Bermuda lawns should be fertilized monthly at a rate equivalent to about 1 pound of nitrogen per 1,000 square feet. Other nutrients, specifically phosphorus and potassium, should be applied based on soil test recommendations. St. Augustine and zoysia lawns should be fertilized at 6-week intervals at a rate equivalent to

Fertilizer	Ratio of plant nutrients	Analysis*			Amount to apply to provide 1 lb. of N per 1,000 sq. ft. (pounds)
		%N	%P$_2$O$_5$	%K$_2$O	
Complete, Balanced Fertilizers					
8-8-8	1-1-1	8	8	8	12
12-12-12	1-1-1	12	12	12	8
Complete Fertilizer					
6-12-6	1-2-1	6	12	6	16
12-6-6	2-1-1	12	6	6	8
6-10-4	3-5-2	6	10	4	16
26-5-3	5-1-1	26	5	3	4
24-4-8	6-1-2	24	4	8	4
Soluble Nitrogen Fertilizers					
Ammonium nitrate		33	0	0	3
Ammonium sulfate		21	0	0	5
Urea		45	0	0	2
Slow-Release Nitrogen fertilizers					
Ureaformaldehyde (Ex. Ureaform, Nitroform, IBDU		38	0	0	3
(Ex. Par Ex)		31	0	0	3
Organic Fertilizers					
Activated sewerage sludge (Ex. Milorganite)		6	3	0	16
Cottonseed meal		6	2	0	16

*Phosphorus and potassium fertilization rates should always be based on soil test recommendations.

1 pound of nitrogen per 1,000 square feet. Depending on the sources of nitrogen used, these rates and frequencies may be adjusted (see the table above). Slow-release and organic fertilizers can be applied in larger and less frequent doses.

Start fertilizing in early spring, immediately following scalping of the lawn, and continue throughout the growing season until the first frost. As with irrigation, the distribution of fertilizer is as important as the rate of application. Uniform distribution may be achieved by splitting the fertilizer into two lots and applying it in two directions over the lawn with a cyclone-type or drop-type fertilizer distributor. In areas where iron chlorosis is a problem, applications of iron sulfate or iron chelate are necessary for St. Augustine lawns. Monthly application of iron sulfate at a rate of 6 ounces per 1,000 square feet may be required in areas where soil pH is 7.5 or higher.

Pest problems always must be anticipated. With St. Augustine grass, chinch bugs and brownpatch problems are to be expected. Chemicals recommended for control of these pests (see page 26) should be applied before conditions favorable to pests develop. Weed problems, such as crabgrass during the summer and clover or chickweed during the winter months, should also be anticipated. Weed and feed combinations that contain fertilizer plus a herbicide can be applied in the fall for control of annual winter grasses and broadleaf weeds.

There is almost no limit to the maintenance you can give your lawn; its ability to enhance the beauty and value of your home is almost limitless, too.

Moderately Maintained Lawns

Common Bermuda grass, St. Augustine grass, zoysia, Bahia, centipede, and tall fescue are all adapted to moderate lawn maintenance. Although automatic irrigation is not required for this level of maintenance, some supplemental watering is necessary. All of these grasses will require occasional watering during mid-summer to maintain color and growth. Watering at 5- to 7-day intervals during the critical mid-summer period will carry these grasses through in good shape. The important thing to remember with this type of watering schedule is to wet the soil to a depth of 4 to 6 inches each watering. A light sprinkle that wets only the surface inch of soil can be more detrimental than helpful. Light irrigation produces shallow-rooted grass, which is very susceptible to drought stress. Of the grasses adapted to a moderate level of maintenance, Bermuda and Bahia are most drought-tolerant, followed by St. Augustine and zoysia; centipede and tall fescue are the least drought-tolerant.

Perforated hose-type sprinklers provide a gentle, even distribution of water.

When you water the lawn, wet the soil to a depth of 4 to 6 inches each watering. A light sprinkle can be more harm than help, since it produces shallow-rooted grass, which is very susceptible to draught stress.

All of these grasses with the exception of centipede should be mowed every 7 to 10 days. Centipede grass can go 10 to 14 days between mowings and still maintain an attractive lawn. Mowing heights for these grasses range from 1 to 2 inches, but under heavily shaded conditions you can raise the mowing height to 3 inches for some grasses, such as St. Augustine and tall fescue. Common Bermuda grass and centipede produce the best looking turf when mowed at 1 inch; St. Augustine and Bahia grasses look best when mowed between 1½ and 2 inches. Again, the shorter you mow the grass, the more frequently it will need mowing.

When you mow at these heights and frequencies, don't remove grass clippings. Instead, leave them to decompose and recycle plant nutrients through the lawn; this will help cut down on fertilizer expenses, too. Of course, when you wait too long between mowings, you'll have to remove clippings to prevent smothering the lawn.

Just as with intensively managed lawns, reduce the mowing height to approximately ½ inch in the early spring, mow in two directions, and collect grass clippings to reduce thatch accumulation

For common Bermuda, St. Augustine and Bahia grasses, fertilization programs should include spring and fall fertilization and perhaps one summer application of nitrogen. (All applications should be at a rate equivalent to 1 pound of nitrogen per 1,000 square feet.) Centipede should be fertilized only in the early fall at a rate equivalent to 1 pound of nitrogen per 1,000 square feet. Fertilize tall fescue in early fall and early spring, with an additional application of nitrogen in late spring. In all cases, phosphorus and potassium fertilization rates should be based on soil test recommendations. Both centipede and St. Augustine will require supplemental applications of iron (as sulfate or iron chelate) throughout the growing season.

Accurate *identification* of pest problems and the application of recommended pesticides is essential to the maintenance of attractive lawns at any level of maintenance. Refer to pages 19-36 for identification of pest problems and recommended control procedures. *Preventive* pest control programs don't have to be followed at this level of maintenance.

Low Maintenance Lawns

Centipede, Bahia, tall fescue and carpet grasses are the only turfgrasses that should be used for low maintenance lawns. Under a low level of maintenance, other grasses deteriorate and are readily invaded by weeds. Carpet grass, tall fescue, and Bahia will tolerate waterlogged soil conditions, while centipede must be restricted to well drained sites. All of these grasses tolerate moderate shade.

Supplemental irrigation will be required during the mid-summer drought period to prevent severe loss of stands in some years. Where irrigation is not possible only carpet grass or Bahia should be planted. Again, when you water the lawn, do it thoroughly (to a depth of 4 inches). With the exception of tall fescue, lawns under a low level of maintenance should be fertilized every 1 to 2 years in the early fall with a complete fertilizer at 1 pound of nitrogen per 1,000 square feet. Tall fescue should be fertilized each fall and spring. Where the soil is inherently fertile, carpet grass lawns may not require supplemental fertilization.

Mow at a height of 2 inches every 2 weeks; in some cases, you can wait longer. You can keep your lawn looking its best with a yearly application of fertilizer and by mowing and edging more often.

Pest Prevention & Control

Lawn pests, including insects, diseases and weeds, cause millions of dollars in damages to lawn grasses throughout the South. Perhaps the favorable temperature and moisture conditions give pests an advantage over the grasses. Also, the widespread use of vegetatively propagated turfgrasses (St. Augustine, zoysia, Bermuda, etc.) here has aided the development of major insects and disease pests. This propagation of uniform plant material for many years has given pests time to adapt to the grasses. Only recently have we seen the production of new varieties of St. Augustine and Bermuda grasses that possess natural resistance to these pests. Floratam St. Augustine grass, for example, is resistant to the southern lawn chinch bug which, alone, has caused millions of dollars damage to common St. Augustine grass lawns.

Today, lawn pest management programs must consist of a better approach than shotgun pesticide application. In Dallas alone, over 300,000 pounds of pesticides are applied annually to lawns and gardens for pest control. Although pesticides can be effective and may be necessary, they only provide a temporary solution to the problem. The basic cause of the pest problem—whether it be poor selection of grasses, poor drainage, thatch accumulation, shade, or improper mowing, watering or fertilizing practices—must be corrected to prevent or reduce the recurrence of the problem. Accurate diagnosis of pest problems is also essential to avoid unnecessary applications of pesticides and to allow timely applications when required.

INSECTS

Insects are a major pest problem to homeowners in the South. Favorable temperature and moisture conditions create environments so hospitable to some insects, such as the chinch bug, sod webworm, and armyworm, that they produce three or more generations each year. By the third generation, large populations of the insects have developed and can wreak extensive damage on lawns.

One serious limitation homeowners face is the lack of information to accurately diagnose insect problems *before* extensive damage occurs. Usually, by the time the problem is recognizable the damage is already extensive and applications of insecticides are not effective. The following discussion of specific lawn insects will provide diagnostic hints on insect identification, cultural recommendations to reduce insect problems, and chemical control recommendations where other methods fail to control insects.

The Southern Lawn Chinch Bug

The chinch bug is a major pest of St. Augustine grass lawns in the South, particularly along the Gulf Coast. In Texas and Florida, the chinch bug is the number one lawn pest problem. In Florida more than $50 million is spent annually to control this insect, and many homeowners have switched to another grass rather than fight the insect.

The adult chinch bug is about ⅙ to ⅕ of an inch long. It is black with white patches on the wings which fold over its back. The nymphs (immature chinch bugs) are much smaller, reddish in color, and have a white band across their back. With each molt the nymphs more closely resemble the adults.

The nymphal stages of the insect cause most of the damage observed on lawns. The insects have sucking mouthparts and feed by extracting the juices from the grass. Damage first appears as small yellow or brown discolored areas that increase in size as the insect population increases. The chinch bugs migrate from damaged and dead grass to healthy grass in irregular patterns. Thus, there is not a distinct boundary or pattern to

Insects that Damage Southern Lawns— Identification Key

I. Insects that feed on foliage

A. Foliage appears cut off or chewed

    1. Damage appears in small circular spots about the size of a quarter, foliage is cut off at the soil level.

       a. Cobweb-like growth can be seen covering the spot in early morning hours, small tunnel or burrow in the center of the damaged spot ....*Sod webworms*

       b. Cobweb-like growth not apparent ....*Cut worms*

    2. Damage appears in large patches, grass blades have a white, skeletonized appearance ....*Armyworms*

B. Foliage appears chlorotic and wilted as though suffering drought or nutrient deficiency.

    1. Close observation of the turf at the soil level shows small, black insects (about ⅛ inch long) with white patches on its wings which fold over its back ....*Chinch bugs*

    2. Close observation of the turf shows small round insects with a white, cottony covering found at the base of the leaf between the leaf sheath and the stem ......*Rhodesgrass scale*

    3. Close examination of the damaged turf shows a stunted growth pattern—very short internodes and short leaves giving the grass a tufted appearance ......*Bermuda grass mites*

II. Insects that feed on grass roots

A. Turf appears wilted and chlorotic

    1. Patches of grass can be easily lifted by hand, fleshy white insects about 1½ inches long usually in a curled position can be found in the top 2 inches of soil ....*White grub*

    2. The grass cannot be easily lifted, small globular insects about ⅛ inch in diameter that resemble a pearl are attached to the roots ....*Ground pearl*

B. Turf is uprooted by small tunnels or burrows along the soil surface, causing the soil to dry and the grass to wilt ....*Mole crickets*

III. Insects found in the lawn that do not damage turf

A. Insects too small to be seen but they become embedded in skin and cause intense itching and irritation ....*Chiggers*

B. Insects about ⅛ inch long, tan to dark brown, oval-shaped, with hard, smooth skin. Insect inserts its mouthparts into the skin of man and pets ....*Ticks*

The life cycle of the chinch bug from larva (left) to nymph (center) to adult (right).

define the population. This first discoloration caused by the chinch bug may be confused with several lawn disease or nutritional problems. Chinch bug infestations can be accurately diagnosed only if the insects are found to be present in damaging numbers.

When damage is severe, the chinch bugs are plentiful and can be found by careful observation of the grass. When the symptoms are first observed a "flotation count" procedure can be used to detect the bugs. A 1-gallon can or a large coffee can with both ends cut out can be pushed through the turf and into the soil at the edge of the yellowing grass. The can should be nearly filled with water for about 5 minutes. If chinch bugs are present, they will float to the surface. If you find 20 or more chinch bugs per square foot in several locations in the lawn, the entire lawn should be treated.

Flotation method of detecting chinch bugs in a lawn.

Insecticides can be applied as a spray or a granule depending on the application equipment you may have and the formulation of material purchased. For effective chinch bug control, soak the lawn thoroughly prior to treatment. Apply the insecticide uniformly over the entire lawn and then water again. Allow the lawn to dry thoroughly before permitting children or pets to play on the grass. If chinch bug infestations are heavy, retreatment may be required in 4 to 6 weeks.

Chinch bug damage usually appears in St. Augustine lawns between June and September. It always develops in open areas of the lawn that receive maximum sunlight and usually originates along a walk or curb or around a building. The chinch bugs overwinter as adults and are more likely to survive in protected areas that obtain heat or warmth from the concrete walk, curb or building. The presence of a thatch layer also favors the survival of the chinch bug as it provides protection from cold, wet conditions. Thus thatch removal and control provides a cultural method for chinch bug control. Also, Floratam St. Augustine can be transplanted into chinch-bug-damaged lawns since it is resistant to this insect. Floratam may require a year or more to fill in the damaged area, but it will spread and provide future protection against chinch bug injury. If chinch bugs are found, they can be controlled with applications of Aspon®, diazinon, ethion or Trithion®.

Chinch bug damage on St. Augustine lawn (note irregular cover, light areas).

Another cultural practice that favors the chinch bug is summer fertilization with soluble nitrogen fertilizers. These fertilizers create succulent growth that is more susceptible to chinch bug attack. If the lawn must be fertilized in the summer, use an organic or slow-release fertilizer.

Chinch bugs are often reported on Bermuda grass lawns. However, close examination of the insects by a specialist will reveal that the insects are either false chinch bugs or big-eyed bugs. Both of these insects are beneficial and will not damage the grass. Chinch bugs have not been found to damage Bermuda grass lawns.

White Grub

White grub are the larvae of several species of beetles. The grub are white with dark brown heads, and they usually lie in the soil in a curled position. The larvae hatch from eggs laid in the ground by female beetles and may stay in the soil for 1 to 3 years, depending on the species of beetle.

White grub as they appear in soil (approximately 1½" long).

In mild weather the larvae are active 1 to 3 inches below the surface of the soil, but they burrow deeper during winter. The larvae (white grub) feed on grass roots about an inch below the surface of the soil. During late summer and early fall, moles, armadillos, skunks, and birds feed on the grub and may tear up the turf searching for them. Large numbers of grub feeding on grass roots cause the lawn to turn yellow and eventually brown in irregular patches. Positive identification of the damage is possible when the damaged grass can be lifted easily by hand from the ground. Sometimes damage is so severe that large areas of turf can be rolled up like a carpet.

Damage from white grub is not restricted to any one grass species. Unlike the chinch bug, the grub feed on St. Augustine, Bermuda grass, centipede, zoysia and other turfgrasses in the South. This root-feeding insect incurs multimillion-dollar losses each year.

Lawns suspected of being infested with grub should be examined in late July or early August. White grub populations can be detected by digging up 1-square foot sections of turf and examining the sod and soil to a depth of 4 inches. After examining the turf, it may be put back in place, pressed down and watered. Treatment with a recommended insecticide is usually justified when more than four grubs per square foot are found in several locations in the lawn.

Unnecessary insecticide applications can create more problems than they solve: repeated applications of insecticides can contribute to grub resistance to chemical control; these insecticides also destroy beneficial soil insects such as earthworms and other organisms that help decompose organic matter.

Insecticides recommended for grub control are much less effective against eggs and large larvae than against small grubs. Therefore, insecticides applied too early may not be effective in the soil after the eggs hatch; insecticides applied too late, after the larvae are too big, generally provide poor control. Lawns found harboring damaging populations of white grub should be treated in late July or early August. This critical treatment period occurs about 30 days after the major flight of the adult beetles. During the major flight period large numbers of adult beetles congregate around street lights or outdoor lights around buildings. There are about three species of beetles whose grub damage lawns in the South: the June beetle, the Japanese beetle, and the masked chafer.

The *June beetle*, common throughout the South, is about ½ to ⅝ inches long with brown leathery wings and head. The major flight for these beetles lasts about 10 days and usually occurs in late June to mid-July.

Japanese beetles usually appear on the foliage of trees and shrubs, around the third week of June. They are not attracted to light like the June beetle or masked chafer. The Japanese beetle is about ⅓ inch long and ¼ inch wide with a metallic-green head and abdomen and coppery-brown wings.

The *masked chafer* is a chestnut-brown color and is covered with fine hairs. Like the June beetles, the adult chafers are night fliers and are attracted to lights. However, only the male beetles are attracted to lights, and since the damage is caused by the larvae produced by the females, lawn damage is not necessarily associated with lighted areas.

All of the female beetles lay eggs in the upper 2 to 5 inches of soil, where the young larvae hatch and begin feeding on roots of grasses and other organic material. As the grub increase in size they work their way close to the soil surface where they feed ravenously on grass roots. During this heavy feeding period the grubs accumulate body fats and become quite resistant to chemicals. During the winter the grub burrow several inches deeper in

the soil to rest. In the spring the larvae feed for a short period, undergo another resting period, and emerge from the soil as beetles in June or July to renew the cycle.

Chemical control can be achieved during the critical treatment period with diazinon or Dursban® (follow label instructions). Since the grub are several inches deep in the soil, the insecticide must be watered in thoroughly. The key to control is proper timing of the application and getting the chemical in contact with the grubs in the soil. Keep children and pets off the lawn until the insecticide has been thoroughly watered into the soil.

Alternative methods of grub control are being investigated, but thus far only limited success has been achieved. Methods that show some promise include the use of resistant grasses, the use of bacteria which attack only the grub, and the use of carefully timed irrigations to prevent female beetles from laying eggs. One bacteria, the milky spore bacteria, is currently available but is only effective against the larvae of the Japanese beetle.

Sod Webworms

The sod webworm is the larval stage of the lawn moth. It is a destructive pest of many turfgrasses during the warm spring and summer months. The lawn moth is about ¾ inch in length and light colored. While resting, the wings of the lawn moth are folded closely about the body. The moth is most apparent during the early evening hours, when they can be seen fluttering above the lawn. The females scatter eggs over the lawn. The lawn moths are attracted to dark green lawns to lay their eggs. Thus, some grasses with an inherent dark green color are most susceptible to infestations, as are lawns that have been fertilized heavily during the summer.

The sod webworm feeds only at night and lives in silken-covered burrows in the turf during the day. It is a light brown color, with a dark brown head, and is about ¾ inch long when mature. The sod webworm chews off blades of grass around the burrow and eats them at night. Damage can be readily distinguished by the circular pattern of cut grass around the burrow or tunnel. Also, in the early morning hours, the silken webs can be readily seen covering the small burrow and eaten area around it. The webworms prefer dry areas of the lawn that receive full sunlight; shaded areas are seldom attacked. The sod webworms also prefer newly planted lawns. Although they will attack most species of turfgrasses, they are a serious pest of the hybrid Bermuda grasses, particularly Tifgreen and Tifdwarf.

You can find the sod webworms by digging into the turf with a spade to a depth of about 3 inches. You can also force the webworms to the surface by applying a drench containing 2 ounces of 2% pyrethrum per quart of water. This drench should be applied to a 2 x 2-foot area of turf. If 6 to 8 sod webworms are found within a one-square-foot section of turf, chemical treatment is indicated. Mow the lawn prior to chemical treatment. If you use a granular insecticide, follow the application with a light watering. When spray formulations are used, water the lawn well prior to application. For maximum effectiveness, apply the insecticide late in the evening.

Fall Armyworm

The fall armyworm can be a very destructive pest to lawns, particularly Bermuda grass lawns. Most severe outbreaks of the fall armyworm occur following cool, wet periods. The young larvae feed mostly on tender leaves, but as they mature they will devour all foliage except the stems. Damage is readily recognized by the white, skeletal appearance of the grass leaves when the insects are active in large numbers.

Newly hatched larvae of the fall armyworm are white with black heads. Their bodies darken as they grow, and full-grown larvae are 1½ inches long. The fall armyworms are greenish colored with dark stripes along each side and down the center of the back. The front of the head is marked with an inverted "Y."

Female moths of the fall armyworm lay eggs on blades of grass or other foliage in clusters of 50 to several hundred. Eggs hatch in 2 to 4 days, and the larvae are full-grown in 2 or 3 weeks. The mature

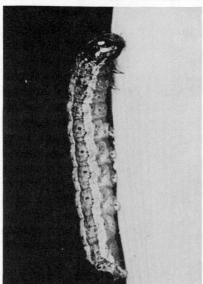

Fall armyworm on grassleaf blade.

larvae burrow into the soil and emerge as moths in 10 days to 2 weeks. Thus, a new generation of fall armyworms may occur in 4 to 5 weeks, and there may be as many as six generations in a year.

Control of the fall armyworm is similar to that for the sod webworm. Control measures should be taken when damage symptoms are apparent and as many as 4 or 5 worms per square foot can be found.

Cutworms

Cutworm damage is similar to that of the sod webworm. The cutworms remain in the soil or thatch during the day and feed on grass foliage during the night. The cutworms chew off the grass leaves and stems near the soil level and the grass takes on a ragged appearance. They are brown or nearly black worms and are 1½ to 2 inches long. Cutworms are the larvae of a night-flying moth that may lay 500 eggs over a 2- to 3-week period. The eggs hatch within several days and the larvae begin feeding immediately. Cutworms can do severe damage to newly planted lawns. Control measures are similar to those for armyworms and sod webworms.

Scale Insects

Scale insects attach themselves to the stems or roots of grasses and suck the juice from the plant. Heavy infestations of scale insects cause extensive damage to lawns during dry periods. Several kinds of scale insects damage Bermuda, St. Augustine, and centipede grass lawns from South Carolina to California.

Rhodesgrass scale can cause extensive damage to Bermuda and St. Augustine grasses. The adult scale is about ⅛ inch in diameter, round, and covered with a white cottony secretion. The scales attach themselves to the base of a plant (crown) with their mouthparts and suck out the juice. The first larval stages of the scale insect are called "crawlers," and they move readily about the grass. These crawlers wedge themselves beneath a leaf sheath at a node or in the crown of a grass plant and insert their mouthparts into the plant. At this time the crawlers lose their legs, appendages, and antennae, and they secrete a waxy covering for protection. In this stage the scales are essentially immune to chemical control measures. Infested lawns must be treated several times at short intervals so that the "crawler" stage of the insect can be eliminated. Management of the lawn to promote recovery would also alleviate the symptoms of scale damage. Heavily infested lawns become yellow and may die if dry conditions prevail. Close examination of the turf at the soil level is required to find Rhodesgrass scale insects.

The *ground pearl* is another scale insect that damages Bermuda and centipede grasses throughout the South. The larvae of the ground pearl attach themselves to the roots of grasses and suck the plant juices. The larvae are about ⅛ inch in diameter and secrete a hard globular covering that resembles a tiny pearl. Lawns infested with ground pearls appear chlorotic, wilted, and generally unthrifty. Close examination of the roots of the grass will reveal the presence of the ground pearl.

Bermuda Grass Mites

The mites are too small to be seen without magnification, but the damage they cause is evidence enough. The mites are a serious pest on Bermuda grass lawns from Arizona to Florida. The mites feed on the grass stems beneath the leaf sheath. The females lay eggs in these protected areas of the plant and can multiply rapidly. Heavy

Scale insects attach themselves to stems or roots of grasses and suck juices from the plant. Rhodesgrass, shown here, can do extensive damage on St. Augustine and Bermuda grasses.

Toxicity Category for Labels on Insecticides

Toxicity category	Signal words required on label by EPA	ORAL LD$_{50}$ (Mg/Kg)	DERMAL LD$_{50}$ (Mg/Kg) 24-hr exposure	Probable lethal dose for adult humans
I. Highly Toxic	DANGER, POISON, plus Skull & Crossbones Symbol	0 to 50	0 to 200	A few drops to 1 tsp.
II. Moderately Toxic	WARNING	>50 to 500	>200 to 2000	1 tsp. to 2 tbsp.
III. Slightly Toxic	CAUTION	>500 to 5000	>2,000 to 20,000	1 oz. to 1 pt. (1 lb.)
IV. Low Toxicity	None	>5,000	>20,000	1 pt. (1 lb.) or more

Classification of Insecticides Used to Control Turf Insects, and Their Toxicity Categories

Insecticide	Classification	Toxicity category
Aspon	organic phosphate	II
carbaryl (Sevin)	carbamate	III
diazinon (Spectracide)	organic phosphate	II
chlorpyrifos (Dursban)	organic phosphate	II
Dicofol (Kelthane)	chlorinated hydrocarbon	II
ethion	organic phosphate	I
lindane	chlorinated hydrocarbon	II
chlordane	chlorinated hydrocarbon	II
carbophenothion (Trithion)	organic phosphate	I
Trichlorfon (Dylox)	organic phosphate	II

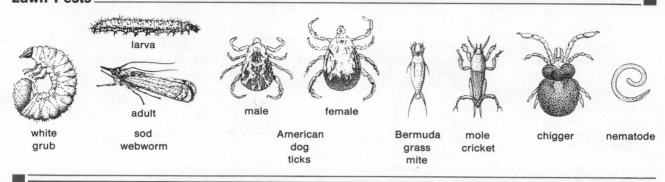

larva

adult

male

female

white
grub

sod
webworm

American
dog
ticks

Bermuda
grass
mite

mole
cricket

chigger

nematode

infestations of mites cause chlorotic, wilted patches in Bermuda grass lawns. Under stress condition such as drought or low fertility, the grass turns brown and looks very ragged. Close examination of the damaged patches will show a stunted growth pattern—very short internodes and short leaves giving the grass a tufted appearance. Weeds often invade the damaged areas of the lawn.

Tifway Bermuda grass, a variety well suited for lawns, has shown good resistance to the Bermuda grass mite. Either dust or spray materials can be used to obtain control. Sulfur dust should be used at a rate of 10 pounds per 1,000 square feet. Insecticides should be applied at recommended rates at 10- to 14-day intervals for effective control.

Bermuda grass mite damage (note tufts of Bermuda grass).

Mole Crickets

The mole cricket is a burrowing insect that feeds on grass roots. In addition, their burrowing up-roots seedling grasses and causes the soil to dry quickly. One mole cricket can damage several yards of a newly seeded lawn in a single night. These insects are numerous throughout the South.

The adult mole cricket is about 1½ inches long, light brown in color, with short, claw-like front legs. Effective control with insecticides requires early diagnosis and treatment before the insects mature. Several treatments may be required for satisfactory control. The insecticide must be watered into the soil where the insect feeds.

Chiggers

Chiggers, or redbugs, are tiny pests that do not damage grass but which are very troublesome to humans. The larval stage of the pests cling to the tips of grass leaves and crawl onto the host upon contact. The chigger finds a suitable location on the host, such as a skin pore or hair follicle, and attaches its mouthparts in the opening. It does not penetrate and burrow into the skin as is commonly believed. Skin tissue becomes reddened and swollen and itches intensely for several days.

When suffering from chigger bites, take a soapy bath as soon as possible and apply an antiseptic to each of the welts. Killing the chiggers does not stop the itching, which is caused by fluid the chigger injects into the skin. Normally, 2 to 3 days pass before the itching stops. Temporary relief can be obtained from one of several commercial products containing a mild local anesthetic.

Control of chiggers in lawns can be obtained with several insecticides, but repellents sprayed or dusted on socks and trousers are more practical. The chiggers are most active during the spring and summer months on Bermuda grass lawns.

Ticks and Fleas

Like chiggers, these pests are found in lawns in association with pets and other animals. Ticks and fleas are parasites of warm-blooded animals and their bites can cause severe irritation and pain and can introduce disease-causing organisms into the

Chemical Control of Insects

Insect	Insecticides	Remarks
Armyworms, cutworms and sodwebworms	Sevin (Ortho Sevin Dust) Diazinon (Spectracide, Ferti-lome Insect Spray, Best Diazinon Insect Spray) Dursban (Best Lawn and Insect Spray, Ortho Lawn Insect Spray) Dylox	Evening applications are preferred. Do not water or mow lawns for 48 hours.
Chinch bugs	Aspon (Ortho Chinch Bug Spray, Ferti-lome Chinch Bug Killer) Trithion (Greenlight Chinch Bug Control) Diazinon Dursban	Apply when damage appears. Water before and after treatment with granular materials.
White grub	Diazinon Dursban (for larvae of Japanese beetle and European chafer)	Drench with water after treatment. Treat in mid-June to early August.
Bermuda grass mites	Trithion Diazinon Kelthane	Use spray formulations and wet grass thoroughly using 3 to 5 gallons water per 1,000 square feet
Ants	Diazinon (Ortho Diazinon granules) Chlordane (Greenlight Chlorane Dust, Ortho Chlordane Dust)	Spot treat mounds or nesting areas only.
Chiggers (redbugs), Ticks and Fleas	Sulfur (Ferti-lome Dusting Sulfur) Sevin Diazinon Malathion (Ortho or Ferti-Lome Malathion)	Repellents are effective and more practical when visiting parks and other recreational areas.
Mole crickets	Diazinon Dursban	Successful control requires early spring treatment when the insects are small.

Mention of a trademark or a proprietary product does not constitute a guarantee or a warranty of the product by the authors and does not imply its approval to the exclusion of other products that also may be suitable.

host. These pests may be found in shaded areas of the lawn and will attach themselves to humans and pets on contact. When feeding on a host, the tick makes a small incision in the skin and inserts its barbed mouthparts to remove blood. The bite is seldom felt, but the wound can become irritating and painful. Early removal of the mouthparts of the pest from the host is imperative to prevent infection. Mouthparts left in the skin can transmit disease or cause secondary infection. To remove the tick with its mouthparts, touch the tick with a hot needle or a few drops of alcohol. Sometimes the tick can be removed intact with tweezers or fingers with a slow, steady pull. Always treat the wound with a germicidal agent.

If tick or flea infestations occur, treat the lawns and the pets at the same time. Ticks and fleas can be controlled with several insecticides. For control of these pests on cats or dogs, consult a pet shop or veterinarian.

Ants

Ants are more of a nuisance than a pest in the home lawn. They build nests in the ground, and in high populations the mounds can smother the turf. Ants also destroy grass seed in the ground and can prevent good stands.

Some ants bite people and inflict severe pain, and so their presence reduces the usefulness of the lawn. Individual ant mounds should be treated when controlling ant populations.

LAWN DISEASES

Discolored grass, thin turf, dead spots, slow spring recovery, and unthrifty turf are symptoms of lawn diseases that cause extensive damage each year. These symptoms are similar to those produced by insect infestations, nutrient deficiencies or other cultural problems. Accurate diagnosis

Southern Lawn Diseases— Identification Key

I. Lawn affected in distinct patches

  A. Individual patches 2 to 3 inches in diameter, leaf lesions on the end of blades ....*Dollar Spot*

  B. Individual patches larger than 2 to 3 inches in diameter. Leaf lesions not present.

    1. Mushrooms present in circular pattern ....*Fairy Ring*

    2. Mushrooms not present in circular pattern.

      a. Grass blades matted together in affected area, greasy appearance, cottony appearance in early morning hours ....*Pythium blight*

      b. Outer edge of circular patch is yellowish-brown in color giving it a "smoke-ring" appearance. Grass blades in this "smoke ring" can be easily pulled from the stem ....*Brown patch*

      c. Circular, doughnut-shaped patches no more than 2 feet in diameter, chiefly on tall fescue lawns in the South ....*Fusarium blight*

II. Lawn not affected in distinct patches

  A. Spots distinct on leaf blades

    1. Orange or red bumps on leaf surface .. *Rust*

    2. Leaf blades show chlorotic mottling (St. Augustine only) ....*SAD*

    3. Oval-shaped spots with gray colored center and brown margin surrounded by chlorotic tissue .... *Gray Leaf Spot*

    4. Oval-shaped spots, light tan in color .... *Cercospora Leaf Spot*

    5. Small elongated spots with dark brown margins ....*Helminthosporium Leaf Spot*

  B. Spots not distinct on leaf blades

    1. Affected areas appear yellow, thin and generally unhealthy, grass roots appear normal ....*Fading Out* (on centipede grass lawns, ... *Centipede decline*)

    2. Affected areas appear yellow, thin, not responsive to treatment, grass roots stunted, swollen, or blackened ....*Nematodes*

    3. Affected areas covered with gray or black powdery mass of spores ....*Slime mold*

III. Lawn areas covered with green crust or mat .... *Moss or Algae*

---

of lawn diseases is necessary for effective control. Where insects cannot be found associated with the injury symptoms, and where nutritional deficiencies can be ruled out because of previous fertilizer applications or soil tests, the symptoms should be carefully checked against those of the common lawn diseases.

Following recommended cultural practices for specific grasses will reduce the occurrence of lawn diseases. For example, high-analysis nitrogen fertilizers should not be applied to lawns in the summer and early fall, when leaf spot and brownpatch diseases, respectively, are likely to occur. Lawns that are heavily thatched should be renovated to reduce thatch. Proper care of grass that is adapted to local environmental conditions is the best insurance against disease attacks.

Dollar Spot

Dollar spot, also called "small brown patch," occurs in the spring and fall on Bermuda, zoysia, and Bahia lawns. St. Augustine and centipede are much less affected by dollar spot. Low soil moisture and low nitrogen fertility encourage outbreaks of the disease. However, sufficient moisture from dew or watering must be present on the grass for the disease to develop.

The disease causes small straw-colored sunken patches of grass about the size of a silver dollar; hence, the name "dollar" spot. In severe outbreaks these small patches may coalesce so that large areas of the lawn are affected. Close examination of the grass leaves at the margin of the diseased spot shows a characteristic brown band or lesion near the tip of the leaf blade. When dew is present on the grass blades in the early morning hours and dollar spot is active, a white, cobweb-like growth of the fungus can be seen on the diseased spot. This growth disappears as it is dried by the sun and wind.

Cultural control practices include thorough, infrequent watering, application of soluble nitrogen fertilizers, and removing dew by watering lightly in the early morning.

Two applications of fungicide may be necessary to bring the disease under control. Turfgrasses recover quickly if treated with fungicides in the

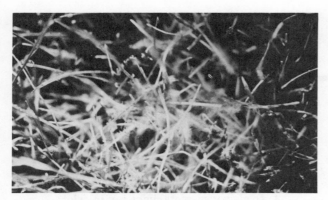
Dollar spot fungus showing cottony growth.

early stages of disease development; if left untreated, the grass may require many weeks to fill in dead areas of the lawn.

Fairy Ring

Usually the first symptom of a fairy ring is a circular or semi-circular band of dark green grass that grows taller than the surrounding grass. This band of stimulated grass is only a few inches wide, but the circle may be many feet in diameter. Often mushrooms appear in the circular band of stimulated grass. The grass within the circular or semi-circular band is usually in a state of decline because of the mass of fungal growth in the soil. The fairy ring fungus feeds on the organic matter in the soil. The stimulation of the grass in the outer edge of the ring is a result of the nitrogen released from organic matter decomposed by the fungus. During dry weather a ring of wilted or dead grass will develop outside of the stimulated band because the fungal growth takes all of the soil moisture.

Toadstools are a symptom of fairy-ring fungus.

Fairy rings are most noticeable during the warm months when the grass is actively growing. Unlike other diseases, the type of grass grown has little relation to the occurrence of fairy ring. In addition, once a fairy ring has become established, it will persist and increase in diameter each year. Control of the fairy ring with fungicides is difficult and requires a combination of aeration and drenching with a fungicide solution at 2 to 3 times normal rates of application. The most effective method of overcoming fairy ring symptoms is to increase watering and fertilization rates. These practices don't eliminate the disease, but they mask its symptoms. The mushrooms can be readily removed by mowing. Positive control of fairy rings can be accomplished by either removing and replacing the soil in the affected area or by fumigating the soil with materials such as Vapam® or methyl bromide. These methods are laborious and expensive and are only justifiable for intensively maintained lawn areas.

Pythium Blight

Bermuda grasses and the cool-season grasses (rye grass, fescue, blue grass) used to overseed lawns for winter color are the major grasses affected by *Pythium*. Grass infected with *Pythium* is rapidly killed in distinct spots that form streaks on sloping areas. In the early stages the grass appears dark and water-soaked or greasy. Later, the grass collapses and appears to be matted together, finally turning brown in the diseased spots. All of these stages may take place within a few hours. When the disease is very active, the affected spots may have a cottony appearance due to the abundance of fungal growth. Because of this latter symptom, the disease is often referred to as "cottony blight."

Warm, humid conditions favor the development of *Pythium* blight. Since the disease develops so rapidly, these conditions need to prevail for only a short period. *Pythium* is difficult to control and requires timely applications of specific fungicides.

Brownpatch

All turfgrasses are susceptible to brownpatch, a fungus disease that attacks the roots, stems, and leaves of grasses. Brownpatch typically produces circular patches of yellow or brown grass that increase in size until treated or until environmental conditions stop the activity of the fungus. The outer edge of the circular patch is yellowish-brown, while the grass inside this "smoke ring" may be green. Thus, the disease produces doughnut-shaped patches of brown grass that vary in diameter from less than an inch to several feet. The grass leaves in the outer edge of the patch, where discoloration is most severe, can be readily pulled from the stem because the fungus rots the leaf sheath that surrounds the stem.

Although the grass may recover from brownpatch, the unsightly symptoms remain until the following spring. Also, winter weeds often invade the lawn in brownpatch-weakened areas. The brownpatch fungus is favored by mild temperatures and moist conditions. It is also favored by the presence of a thatch layer in the lawn. The fungus survives in the soil as a dormant spore, or mycelium, and develops when conditions are favorable and a host grass is present. St. Augustine grass is very susceptible to brownpatch, and the disease usually develops each fall in St. Augustine lawns.

Brown patch symptoms on St. Augustine lawn (note smoke rings).

Fertilization with high-nitrogen fertilizers in the fall, poorly drained sites, and heavy thatch accumulations all favor the development of brownpatch. Eliminating these problems will not prevent the disease but will reduce its occurrence.

Brownpatch can be effectively controlled with fungicides. Where St. Augustine grass is grown and the lawn has a history of developing the disease symptoms in the fall, a preventive application of fungicide should be made when conditions are favorable for the disease. After the symptoms have appeared, the fungicide will stop its spread, but the symptoms will remain.

Fusarium Blight

This disease is a major problem on tall fescue lawns in the South. It is serious only during hot weather, when the tall fescue is weak and under stress. Initially, the diseased patches of grass are 2 to 6 inches in diameter and light-green in color. The spots quickly fade to a straw color and may enlarge to 2 feet or more in diameter. The most characteristic symptom is a circular, doughnut-shaped area with green grass in the center.

If you have a tall fescue lawn, water the lawn thoroughly every 5 to 7 days, fertilize only during spring and fall, keep thatch at a minimum, and mow at a height of 3 inches during the summer months when the grass is under stress. Fungicides may also be used to control the disease after the symptoms appear.

Fusarium blight on tall fescue lawn.

Rusts

Lawns affected with rust have a chlorotic (yellow) appearance and the turf may begin to thin. Orange-colored raised bumps are evident on the grass leaves. If a white cloth is rubbed across the rust-infected leaf, a rust-colored stain will be left on the cloth. When walking through a heavily infected lawn, the rust-colored spores will rub off onto your shoes and pants.

Rust is most damaging in the fall, when grass is not growing rapidly. Zoysia and rye grasses are most severely affected. St. Augustine and Bermuda grasses are attacked but damage is not serious.

Fall fertilization and regular mowing are the best cultural practices for controlling rust. Some varieties of turfgrasses, such as Gulf rye grass, are naturally resistant to rust. Rust diseases can be controlled by fungicides.

St. Augustine Decline (SAD)

Symptoms of SAD were first observed in Texas in 1966 in the Rio Grande Valley and have since been identified on St. Augustine lawns in several southern states. In the early stages of the disease, leaves show a chlorotic mottling or spotting. This mottling becomes more severe and eventually the lawn develops a chlorotic appearance. In the later stages the grass is weakened and thinned, leaves and stolons begin to die, and Bermuda grass and weeds invade the St. Augustine lawn. The various stages of the disease may persist for several years and the grass may survive indefinitely—thus the name St. Augustine decline.

St. Augustine leaf blades—healthy (left), SAD infected (center), iron deficient (right).

Since SAD is caused by a virus, there is no chemical control. In some cases, naturally resistant strains of St. Augustine grass develop in lawns and eventually crowd out SAD infected grass. Also, Floratam St. Augustine grass, which is resistant to SAD, can be transplanted into diseased lawns.

Leaf Spots

Several fungal organisms produce brown spots on the leaves and stems of grasses. Ordinarily, these spots develop in isolated areas, and even then only on a few scattered leaves. However, when environmental conditions are favorable and a susceptible host is present, the disease can defoliate sections of the lawn and severely thin the turf. A healthy, vigorous lawn can withstand these attacks without serious loss of grass. But a heavily shaded lawn, an improperly fertilized lawn, an improperly watered lawn, or a lawn weakened by other conditions can be severely damaged by leaf spot diseases.

Gray leaf spot is a serious problem on St. Augustine lawns, particularly under shaded conditions. Gray leaf spot produces oval-shaped lesions with a brown outer margin and a gray-colored center. The lesions may vary from ⅛ to ½ inch in length and appear on the leaves and stems of St. Augustine grass. Under conditions favorable for the fungus, 30 or more spots may develop on a single leaf, giv-

ing it a burned or scorched appearance. The disease is most severe during the summer months and can severely thin a St. Augustine lawn growing under partial or moderate shade. Open areas of the lawn that receive full sunlight are not immune to the disease, but the extent of the damage is much less. Conditions other than shade that increase the susceptibility of St. Augustine to gray leaf spot include excessive nitrogen fertilization during the summer and late evening watering of the lawn, which keeps the grass moist all night. Gray leaf spot can be controlled with fungicides, but unless the conditions favoring the disease are corrected, control with fungicides is difficult and requires frequent applications. If shade is a problem, reduce it by pruning lower branches of trees or removing smaller trees and shrubs. Often, planting a groundcover is a more practical solution to the disease problem created by shade.

Gray leaf spot on St. Augustine grass.

Cercospora leaf spot was first reported on St. Augustine grass in Florida in 1959. The disease consists of small elongated brown to purple leaf spots. With time the spots enlarge and appear similar to those of gray leaf spot, but are light tan in color. Affected leaves may have a dozen or more spots and will begin to wither and dry out from the tip down the leaf blade, eventually resulting in distinct thinning of the lawn. The disease appears to affect large areas of the lawn rather than localized, small areas. *Cercospora* is most severe in lawns of very low fertility and can be controlled by applications of fertilizer and fungicides.

Helminthosporium leaf spot is another fungus disease that can severely defoliate a lawn. It is a more serious pest to Bermuda grass than to St. Augustine, though it will attack all turfgrasses. The lesions caused by this disease are smaller and darker colored than those caused by gray leaf spot. If the disease persists, the spots on the leaf enlarge to form elongated spots that are tan in the center and dark brown at the margins. *Helminthosporium* is a problem in both spring and fall, when temperatures are mild. *Helminthosporium* can be readily controlled by fungicides.

Helminthosporium *on Bermuda grass.*

Fading-Out

Fading-out is caused by a complex of *Helminthosporium* and *Curvularia* fungi that attack grass when it is already weakened by nematodes, poor management or environmental stresses. The disease is most destructive during hot humid weather. Diseased areas appear as yellow, thin turf that resembles grass suffering from iron deficiency or low fertility. When the condition persists, the grass "fades out," leaving dead grass in irregular patches several inches in diameter.

For effective control, correct the condition that first weakened the grass and follow good cultural practices. Fungicide applications recommended for control of *Helminthosporium* will hasten recovery of affected turf.

Nematodes

Plant-parasitic nematodes are microscopic worm-like organisms that feed on the roots of turfgrasses and other plants. The above-ground symptoms of nematodes reflect the weakened condition of the root system. The lawn may wilt shortly after watering or it may appear to be inadequately fertilized. Fading-out or generally unhealthy turf may result from nematode infesta-

Lawn Diseases and Their Control

Disease	Principal Turfgrasses	Season	Fungicides*
Brownpatch	St. Augustine, Bermuda, zoysia, tall fescue, rye grass	Spring and fall	PCNB (Scotts Lawn Disease Control, Terraclor, Ferti-lome Brown Patch Control, Ortho Lawn Fungicide) Benomyl (Tersan 1991) Chlorothalonil (Daconil) Maneb (Fore, Manzate 200, Tersan LSR) Cycloheximide + PCNB (Acti-dione RZ)
Dollar Spot	Bermuda grass, zoysia, cool-season grasses	Spring and fall	Chlorothalonil Benomyl Cycloheximide + Thiram (Acti-dione Thiram)
Helminthosporium Leaf Spot	Bermuda, St. Augustine, zoysia, rye grass, tall fescue	Fall	Captan Maneb Cycloheximide-Thiram Chlorothalonil
Gray Leaf Spot	St. Augustine	Summer	Chlorothalonil
Fusarium blight	Tall fescue	Summer	Benomyl Maneb
Rusts	Zoysia, rye grass, tall fescue	Fall	Cycloheximide + Thiram Maneb Chlorothalonil
Pythium blight	Rye grass, tall fescue, Bermuda grass	Summer and fall	Terrazole (Koban) Chloroneb (Tersan SP)
Nematodes	All turfgrasses	Summer	DBCP (Nemagon, Fumazone)
Moss and Algae	Bare soil or thin turf areas	Summer	Copper sulfate or ferrous ammonium sulfate

*Mention of a trademark or a proprietary product does not constitute a guarantee or a warranty of the product by the authors and does not imply its approval to the exclusion of other products that also may be suitable.

tions. Careful examination of the root system of the grass will show stunted, swollen or blackened roots.

Nematode-infested turf may respond temporarily to applications of water and fertilizer, but this may only encourage further nematode activity, which will further restrict the root system. Nematocides that effectively control nematodes in established lawns are available, but should be applied by professional applicators.

Slime Molds

Slime molds alarm homeowners when they suddenly appear on lawns in warm weather after heavy rains or watering. They aren't parasitic on grass, but they are unsightly. They cover leaf blades with a dusty gray or black mess of powdery spores that can be easily rubbed or washed off the grass. No chemical control is necessary for the slime molds. Mowing grass usually removes them.

Moss and Algae

The occurrence of moss in a lawn indicates low fertility, poor drainage, high soil acidity, overwatering or too frequent watering, heavy shade, soil compaction or a combination of these factors. Low fertility and poor drainage are the most common causes. Moss can be controlled by applying copper sulfate or ferrous ammonium sulfate at a rate of 3 ounces in 4 gallons of water per 1,000 square feet of lawn. After the moss has been removed, correct the basic problem and follow with good management practices.

Algae can be found in moist areas under trees where it is often mistaken for moss. It, too, can be controlled with copper sulfate spray or drench.

LAWN WEEDS

A healthy turf is the best control for lawn weeds. Broadleaved weeds such as clover, dandelion or knotweed and weedy grasses such as crabgrass and sandbur are usually not a problem where adapted grasses are properly watered, mowed, and fertilized. Weed invasion is most likely to occur where the lawn has been thinned or weakened by pests, environmental stress or poor management. Turf must be healthy and vigorous to successfully compete with weeds for water, nutrients, and sunlight. Once weeds become established in a lawn, they usually have the competitive advantage over the grass because of their adaptive mechanisms for survival. Thus, where cultural practices fail to

eliminate weed problems, herbicides may be used to control them.

Weed Prevention

Regardless of the level of maintenance used on a lawn, sound planning and maintenance can keep weed problems to a minimum in most cases.

- Select a grass adapted for the site.
- Plant high-quality seed, sprigs or sod.
- Fertilize lawns in spring to promote grass recovery and in the fall to prolong the growing period. Such a program produces a dense grass cover that resists invasion by weeds.
- Raise mowing height slightly during summer stress period to help maintain a complete grass cover.
- Control insect and disease pests to prevent invasion by weeds in the areas damaged by the pest.
- Water lawns thoroughly and only when needed. Light, frequent watering keeps the soil surface moist, promoting weed seed germination.
- Cultivate (aerate and dethatch) lawns only when the grass is vigorously growing. Otherwise, weeds will fill in where the grass is slow to recover.

Weed Control

Some weeds may invade or persist even though all the proper maintenance practices are followed. In this case, mechanical or chemical control measures must be taken. Where only a few weeds are present, hand removal is best. But, in the case of the most troublesome weeds, there are usually too many to control by hand.

Effective and safe use of herbicides is dependent on a number of factors: (1) identification of weeds to be controlled; (2) selection of an approved herbicide that is effective on such weeds; (3) consideration of possible damage to the turfgrass, trees, shrubs, and other plants; (4) application at the proper time and rate; (5) uniform application with the proper equipment; and (6) observing label precautions for use.

Identification of weed species is difficult and requires expert training, but illustrations will help you identify the most common weeds. Perhaps the most critical distinction to make between weeds is whether they are grassy weeds or broadleaved weeds. All grasses can be distinguished by fibrous

Goosegrass

Sandbur

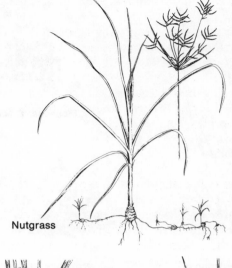

Nutgrass

Crabgrass

COOL SEASON ANNUAL GRASSES

Dallisgrass

Smutgrass

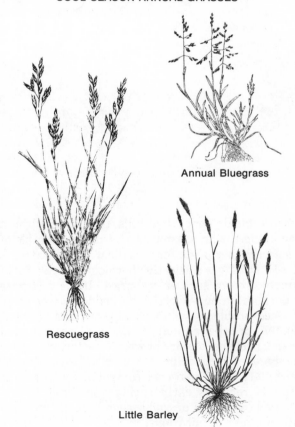

Annual Bluegrass

Rescuegrass

Little Barley

root systems, hollow stems, parallel veins on leaves, and all emerge from seed with a single seedling leaf. Broadleaved weeds emerge from seed with two seedling leaves, the leaf veins form a net-like pattern, and most have a single tap root.

Another important consideration about weeds is their duration—whether they are annual (emerge from seed each year) or perennial (recover from dormant stems or roots). Also, their season of growth (cool season or warm season) can provide a clue to their control.

This basic information is often adequate to select a class of herbicides for effective control. When selecting a herbicide, the stage of growth of the weed (before seed germination, seedling stage, succulent stage or mature stage) must be con-

Mouseear Chickweed

Ground Ivy

Shepherdspurse

Prostrate Spurge

Henbit

Common Chickweed

Dichondra

Dollarweed

White
Clover

Bur Clover

Prostrate
Knotweed

Dandelion

Rugel's
Plantain

sidered. Weeds become more difficult to control with herbicides as they increase in age. The best time to control broadleaf weeds is while they are young and actively growing. Many weeds will germinate in the fall, overwinter in a more or less dormant state, and send up flower stalks or seedstalks in the spring. Thus, the younger, more active growth occurs in the fall, which would be the most desirable time to control such weeds. In the case of summer annuals, spring is the best time to control them with herbicides.

The stage of growth of the turfgrass is also an important consideration when selecting a herbicide. If the turfgrass is actively growing, a selec-

tive herbicide (one that kills the weed without damaging the grass) must be used. An example of a selective herbicide for broadleaf weed control is 2, 4-D. DSMA is a selective herbicide for control of annual grasses such as crabgrass. If the turfgrass is dormant, a non-selective herbicide may be used. If weed problems such as crabgrass, rescuegrass, sandbur or other annual grasses can be anticipated from a previous history of weed infestations, a pre-emergence herbicide may be used before the weeds germinate. Pre-emergence control of warm-season annuals requires early spring applications; pre-emergence control of cool-season annuals requires late summer applications.

Broadleaf Weed Control in Lawns

Herbicide	Product*	Formulation	Remarks
2,4-D	Weedar 64 or Dacamine 4-D	(4 lb/gal) liquid (4 lb/gal) liquid	Do not use on St. Augustine or centipede lawns.
2,4-D + MCPP	Chipco Turf Kleen or Scott's Bonus Type B	(2 lb/gal) liquid 26-4-3 fertilizer with 2,4-D & MCPP granular	Apply to foliage when weeds are young and actively growing. May damage St. Augustine or centipede if applied when temp. is above 85°.
2,4-D + Dicamba	Amchem Super D Weedone Ferti-lome Weed Killer	Liquid Liquid	Same as above.
2,4-D,MCPP+ Dicamba	Greenlight Wipeout Broadleaf Weed Killer or Trimec or Trex-San	Liquid Liquid Liquid	Same as above.
Silvex	Ortho Chickweed and Clover Killer	Liquid	Same as above.
Silvex + 2,4-D	Ortho Weed-B-Gon	Liquid	Same as above.
MCPP	Chipco Turf Herbicide MCPP	(2 lb/gal) liquid	Same as above.
MCPP + Maintain	Ortho Weed-B-Gon for Southern Grasses	Liquid	Same as above.
Endothall	Ferti-lome Clover, Weed and Wild Grass Killer	Liquid	Use only in winter and early spring.

*Mention of a trademark or a proprietary product does not constitute a guarantee or a warranty of the product by the authors and does not imply its approval to the exclusion of other products that also may be suitable.

Preemergence Control of Annual Grasses in Established Lawns

Herbicide	Product*	Formulation	Remarks
Atrazine or Simazine	Scotts Bonus Type S Sta-Green	36-0-0 fertilizer plus .8% atrazine 10-5-5 fertilizer plus .25% simazine	Use on St. Augustine, zoysia, and centipede lawns only. Avoid application within root zone of trees and shrubs. Use lower rate on sandy soils.
DCPA (Dacthal)	Dacthal Ortho Crabgrass Control plus Lawn Food Fertilome Crabgrass and Weed Preventer Heritage House Dacthal plus	75% WP 18-3-6 fertilizer plus dacthal 4.87% 4-0-0 fertilizer 11-4-7 fertilizer with 2.28% dacthal	Use light rate on sandy soils and higher rate on heavy (clay) soils. For use on Bermuda grass, St. Augustine, zoysia, centipede and fescue lawns.
Benefin (Balan)	Vertagreen Weed & Feed for Texas Lawns Zipp Turf Food with balan Gro-Tex Weed & Feed	10-5-5 fertilizer with 0.344% balan 16-5-8 fertilizer with 1.2% balan 12-6-6 fertilizer with 0.25% balan	Same as above.
Bensulide (Betasan or Pre-San)	Scott's Super Halts Plus	32-4-4 fertilizer with 4.5% bensulide	Same as above.

*Mention of a trademark or a proprietary product does not constitute a guarantee or a warranty of the product by the authors and does not imply its approval to the exclusion of other products that also may be suitable.

Non-selective Control of Annual Broadleaf
Weeds and Grasses in Dormant Turf

Herbicide	Product*	Formulation	Remarks
Cacodylic acid	Phytar 560 Contax Weed and Grass Killer	Liquid (2½ lbs/gal.) Liquid	Spray thoroughly to just short of runoff. Avoid spray contact with foliage of green plants.
Endothall	Penco Endothall Turf Herbicide	Liquid	Same as above.

*Mention of a trademark or a proprietary product does not constitute a guarantee or a warranty of the product by the authors and does not imply its approval to the exclusion of other products that also may be suitable.

Grassy Weed Control in Bermuda
and Zoysia Lawns

Herbicide	Product*	Formulation	Remarks
MSMA	Ansar 529; or Mesamate 600; or Daconate 6; or Ferti-lome Crabgrass and Dallisgrass Killer	(4 lbs/gal) liquid (6 lb/gal) liquid (6 lb/gal) liquid Liquid	Spray to wet leaves. Repeat treatment in 10 to 14 days. Treat when soil is moist and temperature is 80° to 90°. Do not use on St. Augustine, centipede, carpet or Bahia lawns.
DSMA	Ansar DSMA	(3.6 lb/gal) liquid	Same as above.
AMA	Super Dal-E-Rad or Ortho Crabgrass Killer	Liquid Liquid	Same as above.

*Mention of a trademark or a proprietary product does not constitute a guarantee or a warranty of the product by the authors and does not imply its approval to the exclusion of other products that also may be suitable.

Control of Poison Ivy and Poison Oak on
Trees and Fences Around the Home

Herbicide	Product*	Formulation	Remarks
Amitrole	Amitrol	Pressurized spray can	Spray each cluster of leaves until you see a sheen on the leaves. Do not spray tree leaves.
2,4-D + MCPP	Ortho Poison Ivy Control	Pressurized spray can	Same as above.
Ammonium sulfamate	Ammate X Ferti-lome Poison Ivy Killer	Wettable Powder Wettable Powder	Spray to wet foliage. Do not spray tree leaves.

*Mention of a trademark or a proprietary product does not constitute a guarantee or a warranty of the product by the authors and does not imply its approval to the exclusion of other products that also may be suitable.

The toxicity of herbicides to turfgrasses, shrubs, trees, and other plants around the home must be carefully considered. Some herbicides are safe on all turfgrasses, while others are highly toxic to some turfgrasses. Likewise, some materials can be used safely around trees and shrubs, while others may not. This information can be obtained by reading the herbicide label carefully before purchasing a product.

The timing, rate, and method of application are also critical for obtaining desired results from her-bicides. This information is also on the product label. You can purchase various formulations of herbicides, including granular, wettable powder, and liquid materials. Granular materials must be applied with gravity-flow or cyclone-type distributors. Distributor settings must be provided on the product label or the spreader must be calibrated to apply the desired amount of material. Wettable powders and liquids should be applied with pressure sprayers by professional lawn service applicators. Don't use small hand sprayers or hose-end sprayers to apply herbicides. Rate and uniformity of application are critical for effective weed control.

Finally, precautions are carefully included on the labels of all pesticides. These precautions *must* be observed to prevent injury to the lawn or other plants around the home, as well as to people.

Special Lawn Problems

Your particular lawn management program, grass variety, environmental condition, and soil can create special lawn problems. Even with good management, problems arise because of thatch accumulation, shade, summer drought, soil compaction, soil acidity, or poor drainage.

THATCH—ITS CAUSES AND CONTROL

What Is Thatch?

How often have you heard a homeowner say that "walking on the neighbor's lawn is like walking on a carpet"? Some people think such a condition is ideal, a luxury. However, the characteristic that contributes most to this luxuriance is thatch—an accumulation of living and dead plant tissues between the soil and the green vegetative cover.

A limited amount of thatch, perhaps ½ inch on an intensively managed lawn, is desirable because it makes the turf resilient and conserves soil moisture. However, when thatch increases beyond this depth, its negative aspects outweigh the desirable ones. Mowing a heavily thatched turf often results in an unsightly scalped appearance, and watering results in excess runoff which carries nutrients and pesticides with it. Not only is water wasted, but fertilizers and pesticides pollute the runoff water that may ultimately find its way to streams and reservoirs. And while thatch reduces the effectiveness of pesticides, it provides a favorable habitat for insects and disease organisms; thus, insect and disease control becomes more troublesome. Also, excess thatch

Desirable thatch level in Bermuda grass lawn.

leads to shallow root systems which increases a lawn's susceptibility to environmental stresses such as drought and winterkill.

What Causes Thatch?

Thatch originates from undecomposed organic residues that accumulate under intensified lawn management. It consists of a layer of stems and roots entwined in partially decayed leaf, stem, and root tissue between the soil and the green leaves. The thatch layer is very fibrous and tough, and is highly resistant to microbial breakdown. Grass clippings, on the other hand, consist of leaf blades which are readily decomposed by soil microbes. As a result, *grass clippings do not greatly contribute to thatch accumulation*. This is contrary to the often repeated recommendation, "Remove grass clippings to prevent thatch accumulation." Vigorous grass varieties, excessive fertilization, over-frequent watering, mowing practices, and extensive use of pesticides all contribute to thatch accumulation.

Two to four inches of thatch will accumulate in poorly maintained St. Augustine lawns.

Grasses differ in growth rate and in chemical composition, and so they differ in rate of thatch accumulation. Hybrid Bermuda grasses, which have a faster growth rate than common Bermuda grass, develop thatch very rapidly. Zoysia grasses have a high silica content, and the fescues have a high lignin content, both of which will slow decomposition rates and increase thatch accumulation.

Fertilization practices contribute to most thatch problems. Excessive application of nitrogen fertilizers, particularly soluble ones, stimulates leaf and stem growth and leads to thatch accumulation. Organic and slow-release nitrogen fertilizers do not increase thatch as much as the soluble nitrogen fertilizers because the former promote a uniform growth response. Although nitrogen sources influence thatch accumulation, the amount of nitrogen applied to the turf has an even greater effect.

Watering practices may also promote thatch accumulation. Since microbial decomposition of thatch requires the presence of oxygen, saturated soil conditions created by frequent watering retard thatch decomposition. Also, intermittent wetting and drying of the thatch layer hastens the physical breakdown of plant tissues, which increases the rate of microbial decomposition. Thus, frequent watering to keep lawns moist favors thatch accumulation.

Mowing heights that promote tillering and rhizome development also favor thatch accumulation. Bermuda grass mowed at less than 1 inch develops thatch more rapidly than when mowed at greater heights. Mowing frequency can also affect thatch accumulation in lawns. Mowing height and frequency should be such that only 30 to 40% of the leaf growth is removed. Long, stemmy grass clippings are much more slowly decomposed than the more succulent leaf blades. The relationship between mowing height and mowing frequency should not be overlooked—the shorter you mow the grass, the more you'll have to mow. Grass clippings that consist largely of leaf blades and are short enough to work into the turf disappear very rapidly. Thus, clippings from turf mowed at the proper height and frequency will not increase thatch.

Pesticides applied routinely for the control of weeds, insects, and diseases may also contribute to thatch accumulation. Long-lasting insecticides such as chlordane are indirectly associated with increases in thatch. Chlordane reduces populations of earthworms and other beneficial insects, and this leads to thatch accumulation. Earthworms are instrumental in the incorporation of organic matter (thatch) into the soil, which promotes its decomposition. Reducing earthworm populations leads to surface accumulation of organic matter—thatch.

Broad-spectrum fungicides used routinely on a preventive schedule may also promote thatch accumulation. These fungicides reduce the populations of both beneficial and harmful fungi. Since the saprophytic fungi help break down organic residues, they are essential to the prevention of thatch accumulation. Specific fungicides which kill only selective fungi do not affect thatch accumulation. In many turf maintenance programs where both earthworms and fungi populations have been greatly reduced, thatch becomes a serious problem.

What's the Solution?

Maintaining a healthy thatched lawn is not impossible, but the problems encountered in mowing, watering, and pest control often lead to lawn renovation. Short of complete lawn renovation, cultivation practices can be used to control thatch. Vertical mowing, aeration, and topdressing, when performed on a timely basis, will control thatch. In addition, other maintenance practices such as fertilization, mowing, watering and pest management must be adjusted to reduce thatch accumulation.

Vertical mowing (dethatching) of a lawn thins the thatch layer and pulls some of the organic material to the surface where it can be removed. When performed on a timely basis, vertical mowing can thin a turf and reduce or prevent thatch. Intensively maintained Bermuda grass lawns respond very well to vertical mowing on an annual basis. Other lawns may require dethatching every three or more years, depending on the grass variety and the level of maintenance. If a heavy thatch is present, vertical mowing alone will not solve the problem.

Aeration increases air and water penetration of the thatch layer and improves conditions for thatch decomposition. The soil cores brought to the surface by aeration also serve as topdressing, which further aids thatch decomposition. The combination of vertical mowing and aeration serves as a method of cultivating a lawn, much like the cultivation of crop residues with a disc or tiller. Certainly, the soil incorporation of crop residues aids their decomposition. Since we cannot disc a lawn on an annual basis, vertical mowing and aeration is the most practical alternative.

Topdressing a turf with a soil or soil mixture aids thatch decomposition by increasing the contact between soil particles and thatch and by retaining enough moisture to sustain microbial activity for longer periods. In some European countries topdressing is the only cultivation practice used to prevent thatch.

Soil activators and inoculants are promoted as "cathalls" for thatch. Some of these products contain small amounts of plant nutrients and microorganisms. Others are promoted on the basis of the "humus" content and the "miracles" associated with adding humus to the soil. The promotion of these products is almost entirely based on dubious testimonials. Research conducted on some of these products has generally not supported manufacturers' claims that they eliminate or reduce thatch. In research conducted in eight southern states in cooperation with the USDA, applications of two of these products at manufacturers' recommended rates did not increase decomposition of plant residues nor did they increase the number or the activity of soil microorganisms. Research conducted on other biological dethatchers has not shown a significant reduction in thatch. However, research *has* suggested that topdressing with a soil or soil mixture controls thatch more effectively than the so-called "soil activators" or "biological dethatchers."

Shaded Lawns Require Special Attention

Shaded lawns require special care to maintain a satisfactory grass cover. That means mowing higher and more frequently, watering more often, giving particular attention to controlling leaf diseases, and removing fallen tree leaves.

Shaded turf is weakened by lack of sunlight and by competition with roots of trees and shrubs for water and nutrients. Thus, grass growing in shade is generally shallow-rooted, more succulent, and less hardy than grass growing in full sunlight. As a result, the shaded grass is more susceptible to drought stress and disease attacks.

To reduce stress and to promote healthy turf, mow shaded grass ½ to 1 inch higher than grasses growing in full sunlight. Also, mow shaded lawns frequently enough so that only one-third of the foliage is removed at each mowing.

Since shaded turf is shallow-rooted and tree roots are competing for available moisture, apply water more frequently during drought stress periods. And, since grass growing in shade is not able to use fertilizer as readily as grass in full sunlight, fertilizer should be applied only in early spring and fall, when the leaf canopy is not fully developed.

Leaf diseases, particularly gray leaf spot and *Helminthosporium*, can seriously thin St. Augustine grass that has been weakened by shade. As a preventive, a fungicide recommended for leaf spot control can be applied to shaded areas at monthly intervals during the summer. Severe disease infestations will require more frequent applications. Treated areas should not be watered for 48 hours.

Chemical herbicides should not be used on St. Augustine grass in heavy shade since they may further weaken the grass and increase its susceptibility to diseases. Trees and shrubs may also be damaged by some weed killers.

In many home landscapes, shade develops to such a degree that grass cannot be maintained. Even St. Augustine grass, the most shade-tolerant turfgrass, requires at least 30 percent direct sunlight to maintain satisfactory growth. When shade reduces light below this level, planting a more shade tolerant ground cover such as English Ivy or Asiatic Jasmine may be the most practical alternative.

Hot Weather Lawn Problems

The summers bring hot, dry weather and the associated lawn problems. The most common problems are dry spots, thin turf, and weeds which result from improper watering, fertilizing or mowing. Before you apply any chemical, be sure that recommended cultural practices have been followed.

Drought stress commonly occurs during summer and shows up as wilted, discolored turf. Unless water is applied, severe turf losses may result. Water thoroughly and infrequently so that when the grass is watered the soil is moistened to a depth of 4 to 6 inches. Mowing heights might also be raised ½ inch to improve drought tolerance during mid-summer.

Lack of nitrogen or iron often contributes to summer lawn problems. Grass with a nitrogen deficiency may have a uniformly pale color and be invaded by weeds. Excessive seed production is another symptom of nitrogen deficiency. Under these conditions a light application of a soluble nitrogen fertilizer will improve lawn appearance.

Grass leaves that have yellow and green stripes parallel to the leaf margins are probably deficient in iron. In this case an application of iron sulfate or iron chelate at six ounces per 1,000 square feet will usually solve the problem.

If a St. Augustine lawn has symptoms similar to nitrogen or iron deficiency but does not respond to applications of either, St. Augustine Decline or SAD should be suspect. Close examination of turf infected with SAD shows a chlorotic mottling on the leaves (see the picture on page 30). As the disease progresses the grass becomes weak, leaves and stolons die, and Bermuda grass invades the area. Good maintenance practices should be continued where SAD is a problem. Also, Floratam, which is resistant to SAD, may be sprigged into the infected area.

Chinch bugs and white grubs are two insects that cause lawn problems during the summer. The symptoms are similar to that of drought stress and insects should be identified prior to initiating chemical treatment. See pages 19-26 for diagnosis and treatment.

Soil Compaction

Compaction results from traffic over the lawn, poor physical soil conditions, poor water quality or low levels of organic matter in the soil. One or more of these factors can create compacted soil conditions that restrict the movement of water, air, and nutrients into the root zone of grasses. The result of a compacted lawn usually is thin turf, numerous weeds, and waterlogged lawns during wet periods. Soil compaction in lawns is concentrated in the upper 2 to 3 inches of the soil; thus, these conditions can be alleviated by mechanical aeration of the soil surface.

Aeration increases the movement of air and water into the soil and increases the exchange of carbon dioxide and other toxic gases between the soil and the atmosphere. Also, the infiltration rate and water retention of the turf are increased by aeration, reducing the frequency of irrigation required. The net effect of aeration is to promote deeper, more extensive rooting of turfgrasses. Other benefits include the gradual disruption of undesirable soil layers that may exist in the soil root zone, improved resiliency, and stimulation of thatch decomposition. Aeration should not be used as a routine cultural practice; aerate only as needed to correct soil compaction and associated problems. The frequency of aeration may vary from annually to never, depending on the amount of traffic, the soil's physical characteristics, and the turfgrass species. Lawns that receive little traffic may not require aeration at all.

Aeration is best accomplished during periods of active turf growth and when the soil is moist enough to permit deep penetration by the tines or spoons. Soils should not be aerated when wet. The aeration operation should be scheduled to avoid the optimum germination periods of serious weeds such as crabgrass.

A number of aeration tools have been developed for turf maintenauce including coring and spiking equipment. This equipment can be rented for personal use or you can contract a professional lawn maintenance company to do it.

Coring. Coring involves the use of a hollow tine or spoon to remove soil cores from the lawn. The size of the core may range from ¼ to ¾ inch in diameter and the cores may be removed on 2-, 4-, or 6-inch centers, depending on the equipment used. The depth of penetration may vary from 1 to 4 inches, depending on the soil type, the soil moisture, and the weight of the equipment. Coring-type aerators are used to alleviate surface compaction, to reduce thatch accumulation, to increase the effectiveness of irrigation, and to increase the resiliency of the turf. The soil cores lifted out of the turf by this method may be

Aeration aids thatch decomposition. Don't *poke holes; use a soil core-removing aerator that removes plugs of soil like these.*

removed or worked into the turf by dragging, raking or brushing.

Spiking. Spiking involves only the shallow perforation of a turfgrass surface by use of solid tines or blades. Spiking should be utilized for temporary alleviation of surface crusts.

The choice of aeration equipment depends on the problem to be corrected. If compaction is the main problem, the coring method is most effective. On the other hand, if surface crusts or thatch accumulation is the main problem, then the spiking method may be preferred.

Soil Acidity or Alkalinity

Soil pH expresses the degree of acidity or alkalinity of a soil. A pH of 7.0 is considered neutral, while any value below 7.0 is acid and anything above 7.0 is alkaline. A soil pH of 6.0 is ten times as acid as a pH of 7.0, and a pH of 5.0 is 100 times as acid as a pH of 7.0. Soils tend to become acidic in regions where there is sufficient precipitation to leach the soluble salts, such as calcium and magnesium, out of the soil; alkaline soil conditions tend to develop in areas that are rarely leached or that are irrigated with water containing high amounts of calcium and magnesium.

Soil pH can affect nutrient availability, solubility of toxic elements, rooting, and microorganism activity. Most turfgrasses grow best under a slightly acid soil condition (6.0 - 6.7). Once the pH becomes too acid or too alkaline, growth can be greatly affected and steps should be taken to adjust the pH to the proper level.

You can correct soil acidity by applying lime. Lime is composed of compounds of calcium, magnesium or both. The most common forms of lime used are calcium carbonate and magnesium carbonate. If the soil is acidic *and* low in magnesium, then it is best to use dolomitic (magnesium) limestone; otherwise, use the calcitic limestone.

Application of lime should always be based on soil test results. The amount of lime required depends on degree of soil acidity, soil buffering capacity, percent base saturation, turfgrass species, and fineness of limestone. Apply only enough lime to correct the acidic condition. Alkaline soil conditions caused by over-application of lime are just as detrimental as an acidic soil condition.

You can correct moderately alkaline soil conditions by applying an acidifying material such as elemental sulfur or an acidifying fertilizer such as ammonium sulfate. Elemental sulfur, like lime, works best when mixed thoroughly with the soil. If the material is applied to an established lawn, don't apply more than 5 pounds per 1,000 square feet. Sulfur can be purchased in a fine powder or granule form. The powder acts fastest. As with lime, only apply enough material to lower the pH to the correct level. The use of an acidifying fertilizer, such as ammonium sulfate, will help to maintain the soil pH at a lower level.

A soil pH of 8.5 or higher is usually caused by the accumulation of sodium in the soil. In most cases, sodium is applied to the soil through the irrigation water; and, where poor drainage exists, sodium will accumulate and produce a sodic soil. To correct this condition, you must provide good drainage so that the sodium can be leached out of the root zone. Before leaching, add some soluble calcium (gypsum) to aid the removal of the absorbed sodium. If the soil already contains high amounts of free carbonates, sulfur can be used to produce gypsum in the soil. If the soils contain no source of calcium (gypsum or free carbonates), then gypsum or a soluble calcium material such as calcium chloride should be added. After these materials are applied, water the soil thoroughly so that the sodium can be leached out of the rootzone.

Wet, Poorly Drained Soils

Wet, waterlogged soils are caused by poor surface drainage, compacted soils, overwatering, or a combination of two or more of these conditions. Lawns require good surface drainage to carry excess water away from the house, walk, patio or garage. On rather level sites, surface drainage may be very limited and may require good internal soil drainage. On heavy clay soils or in low areas, internal drainage may also be quite low. These conditions produce wet, waterlogged soils, and lawns are typically shallow-rooted, compacted, invaded by weeds, infested by lawn diseases (brownpatch), and generally unthrifty.

Surface Drainage. If improvements can be made in surface drainage by adding topsoil, this would be the place to start. To insure adequate surface drainage, a slope of 2% (2 feet per 100 feet) from the house and other structures to a drain (street, ditch or pit) is recommended. If possible, avoid depressions in the lawn around trees or other plantings. Adequate surface drainage should be provided before the lawn is planted.

Open drainage ditches also provide for improved surface drainage, but they are unsightly and less desirable than other alternatives. Where the slope of the ditch is less than 2%, line the bottom of the ditch with concrete to provide adequate water movement. Where the slope is greater than 2%, grasses can be maintained in the ditch. The slopes on the sides of such ditches should be gentle to allow for regular mowing. These open ditches should only be needed for carrying unusually large volumes of water associated with heavy rainfall. They should be dry under normal rainfall conditions.

Subsurface Drainage. Where surface drainage is not adequate and internal drainage is poor, *subsurface* drainage may be required to remove excess water and create conditions more favorable for grasses and other plants. Clay or perforated plastic tile in trenches 18 to 24 inches deep and backfilled

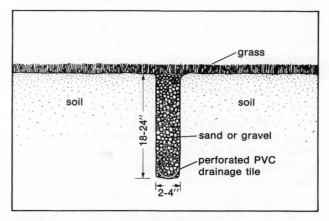

grass

soil

soil

18-24"

sand or gravel

perforated PVC drainage tile

2-4"

Diagram of ditches for tile drain lines.

with gravel or sand provides the most effective method of subsurface drainage. The depth of the trenches will depend on the contour of the land and the soil profile characteristics. On a level site the ditches may need to be quite deep to provide adequate fall or slope (there should be a minimum of 1 foot per 100 feet). If an impermeable layer of heavy clay is underlying a rather shallow topsoil, the trench for the tile need not go deeper than just below the layer of clay. The drain tile system is composed of a main drain line connecting to a series of laterals in a herringbone or gridiron pattern. The spacing of the laterals will vary with the slope of the site and the texture of the soil. On sloping sites the laterals may be spaced 12 to 15 feet apart; on level sites they may need to be 6 to 8 feet apart. Also, the heavier the soil, the closer the laterals must be to adequately drain the lawn. Water moves laterally very slowly in a heavy (clay) soil.

Proper method of installing a subsurface drainage system.

After digging the trenches and placing the tile in the bottom of the trench, backfill the trench with coarse sand or gravel to allow for rapid vertical movement of the water to the tile. The main drain line should connect to an outlet adequate for the removal of excess water. Occassionally, on a level site a pit will need to be dug 6 to 8 feet deep and filled with gravel or crushed rock to serve as a drain outlet.

Another method of subsurface drainage is the "French drain" or slit trench. This method utilizes trenches 2 to 4 inches wide and about 2 feet deep (trenching machines can be rented for this work). These slit trenches are backfilled with coarse sand, gravel or crushed rock all the way to the soil surface. If these trenches are adequately spaced, they can remove water very quickly from the surface of low areas in the lawn. The usefulness of these slit trenches is impaired by soil and grass roots, and their functional life is shorter than that of a tile drain system.

Renovating Your Lawn

Lawn renovation involves cultivation, dethatching, weed control, fertilization and, in some cases, replanting. The most important part of renovation, however, is correcting the problem that caused the lawn to deteriorate. Such conditions as dense shade, tree root competition, low fertility, poor drainage, soil acidity, thatch accumulation, compaction, pest problems, or improper management can lead to the deterioration of a once healthy lawn. All of these problems can be corrected through lawn renovation followed with good management.

After the problem has been diagnosed, follow the practices recommended on pages 26-41. Then, if at least 40 percent of the desired turfgrass still exists, renovation will usually be successful. However, if perennial weeds such as dallis grass or smut grass are abundant in the lawn, and if selective control of these weeds is not possible, then all vegetation should be eliminated and the lawn replanted. If less than 40 percent of the desired grass remains, all vegetation should be eliminated regardless of the weeds present.

Complete Control of Grasses and Weeds

Grasses and weeds can be removed by mechanical or chemical methods. Both methods are best performed by professional lawn service personnel who have the equipment, materials, and experience to do the job.

Mechanical Removal of Grasses and Weeds. Mechanical methods include stripping the lawn with a sod cutter or a tractor-mounted blade or scraper, rototilling the lawn, and raking to remove grass, stolons and rhizomes and, in small areas, digging the grass with a hand tool. After the vegetative cover has been removed, the soil should be rototilled or disked to loosen and aerate, pulverized to break up clods, and rolled to firm the seedbed prior to planting. In some cases it may be necessary to add topsoil to the lawn to balance that removed with the sod. All of these methods require equipment and labor and should be done on a contract basis by professionals. The entire operation could be completed within several days.

Chemical Removal of Vegetation. Soil fumigants such as SMDC (Vapam) or methyl bromide (Dowfume or Brom-O-Gas) can be applied to the lawn

Fumigation with methyl bromide requires a plastic covering.

and covered with a polyethylene tarp for 48 hours. These materials are non-selective and kill grasses and weeds as well as nematodes, insects, and soil-borne diseases. The lawn should be aerated or rototilled prior to their application for more effective penetration of the gas. The soil should also be moist and the soil temperature above 60° at the time of application. Both products enter the soil in a gaseous form, although Vapam is applied as a liquid. Vapam can be incorporated with a water seal instead of the polyethylene cover, but the cover provides the best chance for success. Vapam-treated soils require a waiting period of 2 to 3 weeks after treatment before replanting. Methyl bromide requires only 2 to 3 days aeration time after treatment. The soil should be rototilled after the polyethylene cover is removed to aid the aeration process. Care must be taken that neither of these materials be applied over the root zones of desirable trees and shrubs.

As an alternative to the soil fumigants a non-selective herbicide such as Phytar 560 or dalapon (Dowpon M) can be used to eliminate most annual weeds and provide topkill of perennial grasses and weeds. A single application of Phytar 560 will not kill such grasses as Bermuda grass, dallis grass, smut grass, or Bahia grass. Dalapon will control most of these grasses and weeds, but a 6-week waiting period is required after treatment before the lawn can be replanted. For either of these materials to be effective, the grasses and weeds must be actively growing and soil temperatures should be near 70°. Make sure that the herbicide you use is not harmful to your lawn grass variety or to the groundcovers, trees and shrubs in the vicinity. As with all pesticides, follow instructions and observe all precautions shown on the product label.

Selective Weed Control. Selective herbicides should be applied to eliminate weeds (pages 35-36).

If you cannot identify the troublesome weeds, take fresh samples to your nurseryman or local agricultural Extension office for identification and suggested control measures.

As a general guide, most broadleaf weeds can be controlled with materials such as Greenlight's Wipeout, Ortho's Weed-B-Gon for Southern Grasses, or Ferti-lome's Weed Killer. These products are combinations of several herbicides and provide a wide spectrum of broadleaf weed control. If label instructions and precautions are followed, these products can be safely and effectively used on all warm-season grasses.

If the lawn to be renovated is either Bermuda grass or zoysia, a product containing DSMA, MSMA or AMA (see page 36) should be used along with the broadleaf herbicides. These herbicides will eliminate grassy weeds such as crabgrass and dallis grass. Two or more applications of these herbicides may be required for complete weed control and to kill weed seedlings that emerge from seed after the first treatment.

Dethatching

If the lawn has a deep thatch buildup, it should first be mowed with a dethatching (vertical) mower. This type of equipment can be rented or the operation can be contracted by professional lawn service operators. Again, the clippings and debris brought to the surface of the lawn must be removed. Hand raking the lawn in two directions with a garden rake will accomplish the same task as the dethatching mower, but this should only be attempted on very small lawns. After dethatching, mow at a height of ½ inch and remove all clippings. This may require mowing the lawn several times and gradually lowering the height to ½ inch.

Aeration

To help break up surface compaction and to improve nutrient and water movement into the root zone of the grass, the lawn should be aerated with a coring-type lawn aerator. The aerator should be run over the lawn several times (see page 40).

Lime

Soil tests should be conducted to determine the need for liming and fertilization. Lime should be applied in accordance with soil test recommendations. On sandy soils about 25 pounds of ground limestone should be applied per 1,000 square feet to raise the pH one unit. Clay soils may require 50 pounds of limestone per 1,000 square feet. If the lime requirement exceeds 100 pounds per 1,000 square feet, apply 100 pounds at this time and the remainder in the fall or spring.

Fertilizer

Fertilizer should also be applied in accordance with soil test results. In lieu of a soil test, apply 20 pounds per 1,000 square feet of a balanced, complete fertilizer such as a 12-12-12 or 8-8-8. An additional application of a nitrogen fertilizer such as ammonium nitrate or ammonium sulfate should be made one month after the application of the complete fertilizer.

Topdressing

If the lawn is not level or if small depressions are numerous, topdress it with a loam or a sandy loam topsoil. Approximately 2 cubic yards of topsoil should be spread uniformly over each 1,000 square feet of lawn. The topdressing should be dragged with a heavy doormat, carpet or board to smooth the surface and fill the depressions.

Seeding or Sprigging

To help speed the recovery of the lawn, any large bare area should be replanted. Common Bermuda, Bahia, centipede or tall fescue grasses can be seeded. All other grasses must be sprigged or sodded with vegetative plant material (see pages 13-14).

Water

The seeded or sprigged areas should be kept moist until the seedlings, sprigs or sod have become well established. If replanting was not required, water thoroughly every 4 to 7 days as needed to keep the grass growing. The lawn should not be kept wet, nor should light, frequent watering be practiced.

Sound management practices should follow the renovation program to maintain a vigorous, healthy lawn.

Southern Groundcovers

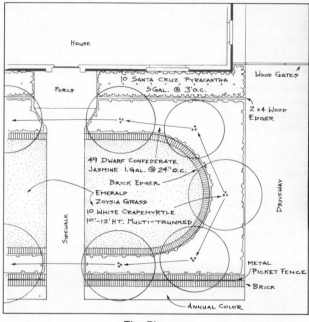

The Plan . . .

. . . And The Results

Most people will know what you're talking about if you mention a "bed of Ivy." Bring up the subject of "groundcovers," however, and you have a lot of explaining to do. A part of the problem is that the term *groundcover* is a classification of various types of plants according to their use in landscape design—that is, to cover the ground. The more familiar basis of plant classification is according to life form (tree, shrub, vine, etc.)

Simply stated, then, groundcovers are low-growing plants of various types used in mass to cover the ground (not all low-growing plants qualify). But the simplicity of groundcovers ends with this definition. Among their ranks are plants from all parts of the world, representing many different families, genera, and species, and with a fascinating variety of forms, textures, and colors. Plants suitable for use as groundcovers may be shrubs, vines, or perennials (including some grasses). Put it all together and you'll find that groundcovers provide a rich palette of materials to add to your garden scene.

Lawns and groundcovers develop their full potential as landscape design elements when used *together*. The fine carpet-like beauty of a lawn is enhanced by contrast with the generally looser, less manicured forms of groundcovers, and vice versa: each benefits in appearance by contrast with the other.

The utilitarian, problem-solving function of groundcovers, although significant, often is stressed to the detriment of their esthetic value. Groundcovers serve admirably for covering bare areas in the shade, on rocky soil, or other areas where grass grows poorly; they're also great for steep unmowable slopes or for helping to reduce long-term maintenance chores. But consider their esthetic design values, too: they can be used to create patterns of form, color, and visual texture on the garden floor or to help create and differentiate outdoor spaces. Or consider their ability to "tie together" many separate trees, shrubs, and garden ornaments by encompassing them within a single planting area, thus helping to bring order and unity to the garden.

Good looking yards and gardens don't just happen—they are accomplished through careful attention to design, selection of plant materials, planting, weed control, and maintenance. All of these are important to the success of a groundcover planting, and each will be discussed in detail.

Designing with Groundcovers

Using groundcovers effectively on your home grounds requires some thought before planting. The best way to organize your thoughts is on paper—that is, draw a plan of your yard. In doing this, you will be able to determine the best location, size, and shape of your groundcover areas and how they relate to other elements of the landscape. Be creative; explore lots of ideas and draw many different, quick free-hand sketches before you settle on one. You'll be glad you did.

Location (Where to Use Groundcovers)

Of all the places that groundcovers can be used, those usually thought of first are areas where lawn grasses will not grow well or are difficult to maintain. For example, lawn grasses usually grow poorly, if at all, under trees casting a dense shade and having many surface roots. In such locations, the right groundcovers can provide a lush covering over the bare earth and exposed tree roots.

Grass would not grow in the shady, root-filled area at the base of this tree. Liriope (Liriope muscari) *provides an effective cover and adds textural interest at the same time.*

Sunny locations sometimes have their problems, too. Areas of rocky or thin, sun-baked soil that support only a scant growth of grass often can be transformed into billowing mounds of growth through careful selection, planting, and maintenance of a groundcover.

Gardeners in those areas of the South blessed with interesting rolling topography sometimes find it a curse when the slopes become too steep. The problem is often compounded by a thin erodible soil and an area that is relatively inaccessible for maintenance. A properly selected and planted groundcover could be the solution. There are groundcovers that can survive and even flourish

Steep slopes require a cover that controls erosion and yet thrives under difficult conditions with minimum maintenance. English Ivy (Hedera helix) *serves well in shady situations.*

under such conditions, covering and binding the soil together to protect it from erosion. Once the plants have formed a solid cover, maintenance on the slope is reduced to a minimum.

There are groundcovers that will do well in unusually wet or dry locations or in those little areas between stepping stones or between sidewalk and street; and many of the available groundcovers will thrive in salty seashore conditions.

Although groundcovers can provide a green covering for many of the problem areas in your

Very low-growing groundcovers, such as Strawberry Begonia (Saxifraga stolonifera), *are useful in tiny areas between stepping stones. Many are aromatic when the leaves are crushed underfoot.*

yard, they cannot cure all of your ills. Groundcovers won't grow well in very dark areas (try a decorative mulch of bark or gravel), or in heavily traveled pathways (use stepping stones or other pavement), nor are they maintenance-free—no plants are (not even plastic plants, if you want them to look good). By all means consider using groundcovers when you have a problem area, but use them wisely.

Groundcovers need not be located in problem areas only. Plants that are thorny or otherwise difficult to walk through can be used to control traffic, routing it where you want it to go. Try using a flowering groundcover with an interplanting of

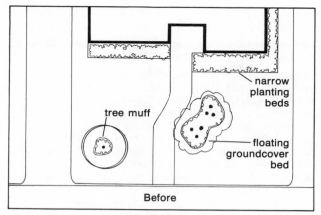

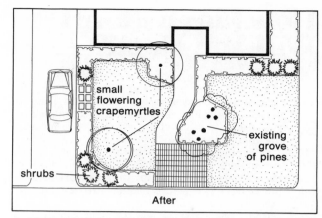

"Small thinking" creates collections of many different and disjointed elements, particularly when only the immediate problem area is considered.

Bold use of groundcovers in orderly, interesting shapes helps unify the design. Here most of the same areas are covered with groundcover as before, and then some. The tree muff is removed to allow the individual tree to be appreciated for its own beauty which is set off by a well defined expanse of lawn. The groundcover beds provide opportunities for the introduction of shrubs to enrich the scene and provide intermediate sized elements between groundcover and trees.

bulbs and shrubs in an area that you see every morning as you eat breakfast. A little imagination and the right groundcover can give you many other interesting design ideas.

In addition to the many design possibilities, there are a few pitfalls to avoid in deciding where to use groundcovers. Be careful not to create groundcover areas that seem to "float" on a sea of grass, with no strong relationship to other garden elements or no apparent reason for being where they are. Avoid the ubiquitous little ring or "muff" of groundcover around a tree. It detracts from the beauty of the tree and adds nothing to the overall design of the yard.

Know the surface drainage pattern in your yard so that you don't place a groundcover bed in the path of the water flow. If the bed is raised, it may cause flooding in areas upstream from it. If the bed is at the same grade as surrounding areas, it may be flooded itself. Mulches may wash away, and if the water flow is rapid enough, plants and soil may be washed out.

Size

One of the primary mistakes many gardeners make in using groundcovers is what might be called "small thinking"—making groundcover beds too small. Be bold, think big. Make your groundcover beds large enough to be a strong design element and to be in pleasing proportion to the surrounding space and to adjacent lawn or pavement areas. Think beyond the typical border along the front walk or the narrow band all the way around the house, or the tree "muff" already mentioned. Think beyond the size of the immediate problem area.

Too often, the economics of the moment determines the size of a groundcover bed. First, deter-

mine the size you want it ultimately to be; then, if your initial budget is small, plant a portion at a time as you can afford it.

Shape

When deciding on a shape for a groundcover bed, consider the area of which it will be a part. Is the area very orderly and structured by the hard lines of house, sidewalk, driveway, terrace, street, or fence? If so, you may need an "architectural" shape reflecting and harmonizing with the straight lines and rectangular forms already there. In a rectilinear situation like that, irregular free forms with many sinuous curves often seem out of place.

On the other hand, gently flowing, simple curves may be just the soft contrast you need. In naturalistic settings, curving shapes seem intrinsically right. In general, the simpler the curve the better looking it will be, particularly in small spaces. An added bonus is that the simple curves are more easily maintained (less lineal footage of edging required, easier to mow against).

Selecting the Right Groundcover

The right plant in the right place is the goal you should strive for when selecting any plant for your garden. This happy situation can be arrived at in your selection of groundcovers through careful ex-

How Many Plants Will You Need?

Here are some suggestions to help you determine how many plants you will need to buy for your new groundcover bed. The main thing to determine is the number of square feet in the area you intend to plant. The first step is to measure the area and to make a square footage calculation. This is easy if the area is in the shape of a square or rectangle. Simply multiply the length in feet by the width in feet. Round off your measurements to the nearest foot before making the calculation—this will be accurate enough.

Oddly shaped areas with straight sides can be divided into a combination of squares, rectangles, and right triangles. Find the area (in square feet) of each part and add them together for the total. The area of a right triangle can be determined by multiplying the two sides forming the right angle by each other and dividing the resulting figure by two.

Circular areas can be figured by multiplying the radius of the circle by itself and the resulting figure by 3.14. This is the well known formula πr^2.

Determining the square footage of free form areas is only a little more difficult. Divide the area into a combination of squares, rectangles, and right triangles and calculate as for oddly shaped areas with straight sides. This will give you a reasonably accurate calculation.

Once you have determined the square footage of the proposed planting area, the next step is to determine how many groundcover plants will be needed. This can be figured for any of several spacings by using the accompanying table. Multiply the square footage by the factor for the spacing you want. For example, a 150 square foot area using a spacing of 18″ apart each way will require 66 plants (150 x .44 = 66). Using this method, you can quickly determine how many plants you would need, and therefore what the cost would be, for several different spacings.

Groundcover Multiplying Factors

Spacing	Multiplying Factor
6″	4.0
8″	2.2
10″	1.5
12″	1.0
18″	.44
24″	.25
30″	.16
36″	.11
48″	.06

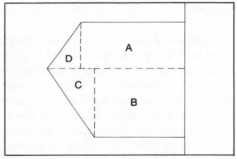

To calculate square footage of oddly shaped areas, divide the area into more manageable shapes as shown by the dashed line.

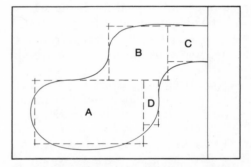

Do the same for irregular, free-form areas.

amination of a list of possible groundcover choices (see chart on page 66), while keeping in mind a set of specific selection factors that you determine.

Because the list of groundcovers suitable for southern gardens is extensive and includes a wide variety of plants, you might believe that the choices for your particular situation are almost limitless. Possibly, but usually not. If you do a good job of determining what environmental and cultural conditions the plants will have to endure, what physical plant characteristics are important to you, and what personal factors are involved, you'll find your choices considerably narrowed. Careful attention to these selection factors can help make the difference between really enjoying your groundcover beds and struggling endlessly with them.

Environmental and Cultural Conditions

In most instances you'll find that your groundcover choices are governed by what will grow in a certain area under the existing conditions, not necessarily what you would like to grow there. To be sure, some environmental conditions can be modified by cultural practices (changing soil pH, regular watering to compensate for dryness, etc.). Generally, however, your choice will be better if you respect the existing conditions and select a groundcover accordingly. The environmental factors of soil, moisture, light (or lack of it), temperature (extremes), and exposure to salt spray, wind, or other potentially limiting environmental conditions in your area will limit your choices to a few likely candidates. From that point, the other selection factors take over to determine your final choice.

One thing you *must* know prior to selecting a groundcover is the nature of your soil. Know whether you have a heavy clay that holds lots of water, a sandy soil that drains rapidly, or some type in between. Find out the pH of your soil (acid or alkaline) and its nutrient composition (how much nitrogen, phosphorous, potassium and how many trace elements it has). If you live close to the sea, know whether or not the soil contains salt, and if so, how much. Your local agricultural Extension agent can provide you with information on how to take a soil sample and the procedure necessary to have it tested by the agricultural Extension service nearest you. Detailed information about your soil is necessary to help you in selecting a groundcover that will grow well under your particular conditions.

Plant Characteristics

Whether you select a trailing or rambling vine, a prostrate or mounding shrub, or any of several types of perennials is, in part, a matter of personal preference. Nevertheless, there are a few things you should know about the various types of plants used as groundcovers.

Some vining groundcovers grow so vigorously that they stay on the ground only under protest. Have your clippers ready for battle if you want to use one of these under trees or shrubs. Otherwise, you will soon find the trees or shrubs under the groundcover!

Shrubby groundcovers that do not root when their branches touch the ground are generally easier to cultivate with a hoe than vines or types that spread by means of runners. These latter may be uprooted by hoeing and are best weeded by hand-pulling.

When considering the size of a groundcover plant or the size of its leaves, think in terms of the size of the space it will occupy. Low-growing, small-leaved groundcovers *(Ajuga,* for example) are better for small spaces than types with very large leaves (Algerian Ivy) or types that grow tall (Rock Cotoneaster). This is partially because plants with large proportions have the visual and psychological effect of making the small space

seem even smaller. In addition, the larger plants simply outgrow small spaces. Conversely, the smaller plants often are not bold enough for use in very large masses or spaces. The solution is to select a plant whose proportions harmonize with the proportions of the space and of the other elements within it (edgings, shrubs, etc.).

Other plant characteristics, such as flower color, leaf color, and density of growth, to name a few, may or may not be of significance in your particular design situation. Consider all of the characteristics, good and bad, of the plants you are considering before making your final choice.

Personal Factors

One of the major determinants in plant choices seems to be economics, unfortunately so in many instances. How much you can afford right now certainly is important, but this should not always be the governing criterion. You can complete your groundcover beds in phases if necessary, and stretch the financial burden over a longer period of time. Another solution is to buy a few plants of a type that is easily propagated, and grow the remainder yourself.

There are several items you should consider in establishing the true total cost of the various groundcover choices. The price of the plant itself is, obviously, first. The plant price is governed by the container or plant size (2½ inch pot, 1-gallon can, 12- to 18 inch spread balled-and-burlapped, etc.) and by the particular plant in question, some species and varieties being more expensive than others of the same container or plant size.

The total quantity required depends on three main interrelated factors: size of plant, spacing, and rate of growth. Groundcover plants in small containers obviously will take longer to grow to maturity and form a solid cover than those in large containers, but the smaller ones are less expensive.

Plants in small containers should be spaced more closely to provide coverage of the ground within a reasonable period of time. The quantity required is larger, thus offsetting somewhat the lower plant price. Plants in large containers can be spaced more widely, reducing the quantity but not necessarily the total cost, since the individual plants cost more.

Fast-growing plants can be purchased in small containers and planted at relatively wide spacings—the cost comes down again. You can easily see the interrelationship of these three factors; obtain all the facts and then calculate your costs using different combinations.

Tips on Buying Groundcovers

Here are some of the containers in which groundcovers are grown. From left to right: plastic tray of Algerian Ivy (Hedera canariensis), flat of Sand Strawberry (Fragaria chiloensis), 2" pots of Dwarf Confederate Jasmine (Trachelospermum jasminoides pubescens) and English Ivy (Hedera helix), one-gallon can of Monkey Grass (Ophiopogon japonicus).

Container Sizes Available

Groundcovers can be obtained in a variety of container types and sizes. Here are the possibilities:

Flats. Thin wooden or plastic boxes (approximately 16" x 16", but sometimes in other sizes) with plants growing in mass. Sometimes the plants are in smaller trays, six or eight to a tray, placed in the flat for convenient handling. Be sure that the flats or trays are filled with plants—you are buying by the flat or tray, not by the plant. Groundcovers in flats must be cut or torn from the plant mass, a method obviously disturbing to the plant, and sometimes to the gardener. More care is required for the first week or two after planting than for plants from pots or cans.

Pots. Found in a variety of odd sizes, usually classified as 2-inch, 2½-inch, 3-inch, and 4-inch, whether they are those exact dimensions or not. More important than the actual size of the pot, since the differences are not great, is the size and state of development of the plant. A full, almost overgrown plant in a 2½-inch pot is usually a better buy than a poorly grown plant in a 4-inch pot.

Cans. Quarts, 1-gallon, and 2-gallon cans are your choices here. Some shrubby plants that can be used as groundcovers may be found in 5-gallon cans. However, because of the large quantities usually required, this is an uneconomical size.

Peat Pots. Occasionally you might find some groundcovers supplied in varying sizes of peat pots (1½-inch up to 4-inch). These are made of sphagnum peat moss compressed into the shape of a pot (square or round). Watch these carefully if you keep them for any period of time before planting, because plants grown in peat pots tend to dry more quickly than in other types of containers. For special tips on planting peat pots, see page 31.

Other Available Forms

Groundcovers can also be found in the following forms or root conditons:

Balled-and-Burlapped. Some shrubby types of groundcovers are sold this way. The plants are grown in a field, dug with a ball of earth around the roots which is then wrapped in burlap or a woven plastic material. Be sure the earth ball is solid and firmly held together by the burlap. The ball size should be approximately 9 to 12 inches in diameter for the plant sizes usually sold as groundcovers. Sometimes balled-and-burlapped plants are less expensive than equivalent-sized container-grown stock. The major advantage of container-grown over field-grown plants is that container-grown plants, if properly handled, suffer much less planting shock, since their root systems are essentially undisturbed.

Bare-Root. Few groundcovers are sold this way, but some may be found (strawberry is one). Plant these immediately and tend them carefully for the first week or two.

Bumming

If you're lucky enough to have decided that the right plant for your place is the same one your friend or neighbor has, you qualify for the use of that age-old method of procuring goods: bumming. The use of this method is contingent on two main factors:

1. The plant must be one that is easily divided (Monkey Grass) or propagated (English Ivy).

2. Your friend or neighbor must be willing to cooperate.

The Encyclopedia of Southern Groundcovers indicates which ones can usually be successfully obtained by this method.

Quality

Quality is sometimes as difficult to describe as morality is to legislate. The plants should obviously be free from disease and insect infestations. Roots should fill the container, but not to the extent of being pot-bound. This is, of course, an ideal—pot-bound plants will certainly still grow. You can facilitate new root growth from pot-bound plants if you make a few vertical knife cuts on the outside of the root ball before planting. Foliage should be full and well-formed. Vines should have more than one runner, each one exhibiting vigorous growth.

Availability

The kinds of groundcovers available will vary from nursery to nursery and from region to region. There are a few that are generally available throughout the South. These are indicated in the Encyclopedia. Your nurseryman can order some of the more unusual ones for you from wholesale groundcover growers in various parts of the country. Most nurseries stock only a limited quantity of any one groundcover because of space limitations, but they can easily obtain more.

Before you finally select a groundcover, consider your maintenance desires and capabilities. Many gardeners plant groundcovers thinking that they will require little or no maintenance. It is true that once a groundcover has formed a solid cover over the ground its maintenance requirement is usually less than that of a lawn, but the initial establishment period of anywhere from six months to two years will find you diligently pulling weeds, spreading herbicides, and perhaps talking to your plants (if not to yourself). Which plant you select can make a difference in the amount of maintenance required. Slow-growing plants will keep you in weeds longer unless you can afford to space them more closely. They may, however, have other redeeming characteristics. Also, some groundcovers form a denser mass at maturity than others and will choke out weeds more effectively, while serving as their own moisture-conserving mulch.

Another factor to consider in selecting a groundcover is whether or not you'll want to grow bulbs, perennials, shrubs, or trees in the groundcover bed. Select carefully so that your final choice is one which will not choke out the bulbs, or cover the perennials and shrubs with mounds of lush growth, or wrap the trees in an entangling mass (or mess) of vines.

Aids in Making Your Choice (How to Use this Section)

Once you've established your own particular set of selection factors, you can use this section to find a groundcover whose requirements most closely correspond. The Groundcover Selection Guide on pages 66 & 67 and the Encyclopedia of Southern Groundcovers (pages 68-86), when used together, will provide the information you need to make your choice. Turn to page 64 for an explanation of these two selection aids and how to use them.

How to Plant Groundcovers

BEFORE YOU PLANT

One question frequently asked is, What is the best time of year to plant? For groundcovers, planting time depends on several things. Generally, spring is ideal: it is cool and often moist—conditions particularly favorable to groundcovers planted from small containers, since these have limited root systems. Also, spring planting allows a full season's growth before the rigors of winter set in. This is particularly important for plants that are tender or slightly so, as they are able to develop strong root systems before freezing weather.

Summer plantings can be successful if they receive adequate water. Groundcovers planted from large containers can tolerate summer conditions better than those in small pots. Those planted from flats will have the greatest difficulty because their roots are damaged the most in planting, so expect a greater mortality rate from flat-grown plants in the summer than from groundcovers in other types of containers. Balled-and-burlapped plants can tolerate summer planting but are best planted in cooler weather.

In many parts of the South, fall brings spring-like conditions and is an acceptable time to plant all but the tenderest groundcovers. In the warmer parts of the South, most groundcovers can be planted just about any time of year if given proper care. But for best results with the least effort, follow the suggestions already mentioned.

Layout

The first step in the preparation of your groundcover bed is to establish its outline. You can use a string line with 12-inch wooden stakes for laying out the straight lines, and a garden hose for curves. If you intend to use a constructed edger of some sort, set the string line or hose about 3 or 4 inches outside the intended edge of the bed. This will give you some working room when excavating for the edger.

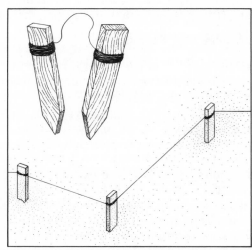

To outline your groundcover bed, use a string line and wooden stakes to define straight areas, a garden hose for the curves.

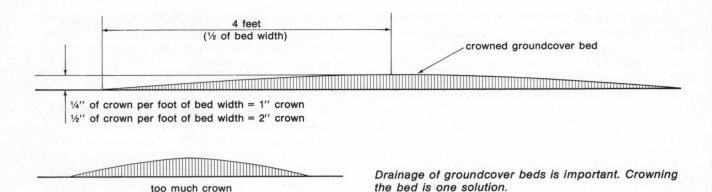

4 feet
(½ of bed width)

crowned groundcover bed

¼" of crown per foot of bed width = 1" crown
½" of crown per foot of bed width = 2" crown

too much crown

Drainage of groundcover beds is important. Crowning the bed is one solution.

Utilities and Drainage

Prior to bed preparation is the time to install any underground sprinkler systems or other utilities that must be routed through the groundcover bed. This is also the time to plan on correcting any existing or potential drainage problems within the bed area. If the ground has a natural slope sufficient to carry water away, you have no problem (other than erosion if the slope is steep). Grade the bed to slope in the direction of the water flow. Be sure the bed is properly located in relation to the overall drainage pattern of your yard (see the discussion under Location on page 46).

On flat ground that drains poorly, the bed must be raised an inch or two and crowned (made slightly higher in the middle than at the edges). How much of a crown to use depends on the size of the bed and the severity of the problem. A good rule of thumb, however, is to use somewhere between ¼ and ½ inch of elevation per horizontal foot of bed width. Don't make the crown too steep or water will run off too rapidly, making watering difficult.

Groundcover Bed Preparation

Materials. Before you get too wrapped up in your work, be sure you have on hand all the materials needed. This is the only chance you'll have to prepare the soil in your groundcover bed, so don't skimp on materials. Your money will be more wisely spent on bed preparation materials than on larger plants.

If the groundcover bed is to be located in an established lawn area, you'll have to remove the grass sod. Along with the sod, you will unavoidably remove a certain amount of soil. Therefore, you'll probably need to add *topsoil* to compensate for the loss. The quantity needed will, of course, depend on the depth of sod and soil removed. A good rule of thumb is to plan on adding about 1 or 2 inches of new topsoil. If, in addition, you plan on raising the bed slightly (say another 2 or 3 inches), figure that into the total quantity of topsoil needed. On the other hand, if you plan on adding large amounts of organic matter, you can reduce or possibly eliminate the topsoil requirement.

Most soils require the addition of *organic matter*, as much as possible, to improve tilth, aeration, drainage, water-holding capacity (sandy soils), and fertility. Generally, a good amount to use is a layer 3 or 4 inches thick over the entire bed area, tilled into the top 6 inches of soil. If the groundcover you have selected prefers a poor soil, you may want to skip this step or use a smaller amount, depending on how bad your soil is. You may also want to limit the amount of organic matter added if you plan on using a herbicide (organic matter reduces the effectiveness of groundcover herbicides; see the discussion of herbicides on page 61).

The material you use will depend on what is locally available in your area. Here are some common organic materials you may find or have on hand:

Pine bark (use the shredded or finely ground forms, not nuggets)
Peat moss
Rice hulls (preferably composted)
Bagasse (sugar cane pulp)
Sawdust or wood shavings
Well-rotted manure (let it sit before using, to germinate weed seeds)
Compost (home-made stuff)
Composted sewage sludge (various brand names such as Milorganite or Houactinite)

Some of these materials will require addition of nitrogen to aid in the decomposition process and to counteract their tendency to rob nitrogen from the soil. The table on page 53 indicates the amount of nitrogen needed for untreated pine bark, uncomposted rice hulls, and sawdust.

Bank sand can be useful in combination with organic matter; it is usually not sufficient by itself. Try a half-and-half mixture of sand and organic

Amounts of Nitrogen Needed with Pine Bark, Sawdust, Rice Hulls			
4-6 Cubic Yards	Ammonium Sulfate (21-0-0) per cu yd	Houactinite (4% nitrogen)	Fish Meal (10% nitrogen) Blood Meal (12% nitrogen) per cu yd
Pine bark (untreated)	15 lbs	75 lbs	30 lbs
Sawdust	7½ lbs	37½ lbs	15 lbs
Rice hulls	3 lbs	15 lbs	6 lbs

matter. Sharp sand (builder's sand) has fewer weed seeds than bank sand, it is coarser and therefore better than bank sand for improving soil structure, but it is considerably more expensive.

Gypsum is often used to improve the structure and thus the drainage of heavy clay soils, but it can be overdone. More is not necessarily better in this case. About 5-10 pounds per 100 square feet should be about right. If in doubt, consult your local nurseryman or agricultural Extension agent for application rates.

The *fertilizer* you will need for your situation depends on your soil's fertility (here's where a soil test comes in handy). Local availability will govern your choices of fertilizer formulations. In general, a complete granular or timed-release fertilizer, not overly heavy on any one element but containing all three (nitrogen, phosphorous, potassium) plus trace elements, will suffice (12-24-12, 10-20-10, 13-13-13, etc.). You might want to consider compressed fertilizer tablets as an alternative. Although your choices of formulation are limited, the tablets are easy to use and are long-lasting (one to two years). Also, each plant receives the same amount of fertilizer, regularly released, for uniform growth. For application rates, follow the package instructions on all types of fertilizers.

If you plan on growing groundcovers that have specific acidity or alkalinity requirements, you may need materials to alter the soil pH. Sandy soils are usually acid (except in arid or coastal regions, where there may be accumulated salts in the soil), and are relatively easily changed toward an alkaline pH. Clay soils, generally, are neutral to alkaline and are relatively difficult to change to an acid pH. Modification of soil pH usually is a continuing process, particularly if the water you use is opposite in pH to the desired change. The best solution is to select a groundcover whose soil pH requirements match your soil's natural condition.

If you want to acidify your soil, *sulfur, chelated iron,* or *iron sulfate (copperas)* applied at 2-5 pounds per 100 square feet will work well. Some organic mulches are acid in reaction and help acidify the soil as they decompose (see the discussion of mulches on page 58). To increase your soil's alkalinity, add *lime.* Follow package instructions or consult your local nurseryman or agricultural Extension agent for application rates of pH-changing chemicals to avoid excessive applications.

One additional chemical you may need, depending on which groundcover you intend to plant, is a *herbicide.* Consult the section on weed control (pages 60-63) for more information.

If you plan on installing some type of constructed *edger,* you will need to obtain these materials also. Consult the section on edgers (pages 54-56) for more information.

Grass and Weed Removal. As previously stated, groundcover beds located in existing lawn areas must have the grass sod removed prior to turning the soil. There are two tools and one machine you'll find useful for doing this. One tool is a flat shovel (the heavier the better) with a squared, sharpened end. Lay the shovel nearly flat and slip it just under the sod, shearing off as much grass and as little soil as possible. This is not easily done, but it works well if you are strong enough. If the grass you are removing is zoysia or Bermuda, you'll have to dig a little deeper to remove as many underground runners as possible.

Another useful tool is a garden adze, a kind of flat-bladed pick (again, the heavier the better). The adze is used to remove grass in a manner similar to the shovel method, except it is swung like a pick. It takes a little practice to hit the grass in just the right place so as not to remove too much soil.

A third solution to grass removal is a rented sod-cutting machine. This machine works most efficiently when the grass being removed is good, solid turf. If the ground is fairly wet, don't waste

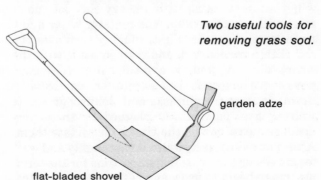

Two useful tools for removing grass sod.

garden adze

flat-bladed shovel

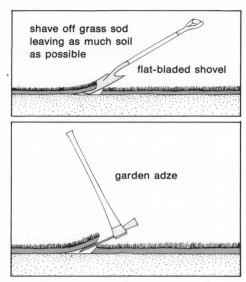

shave off grass sod leaving as much soil as possible

flat-bladed shovel

garden adze

Remove existing grass sod before turning soil.

Rotary tillers work well in light soils, but in heavy clay, soil should be roughly turned by hand first.

your money renting one, because the wheels will merely spin and go nowhere.

If you are working on a new yard with no established turf, remove all weedy growth and volunteer grasses before turning the soil or you'll surely have weed problems later on. Now is the time to get a head start on your weed control program.

Tilling the Soil. The growth habit of the particular groundcover you have selected will have much to do with how you prepare the soil in the groundcover bed. Ideally, the entire bed area should be tilled to a depth of at least 6 inches, and deeper if possible. However, for shrubby types that do not require rich soils and whose branches do not root when they touch the ground, all you need do is prepare each individual hole. This is particularly true if these plants are widely spaced (30 inches apart or greater). Plants of this type are usually planted from 1-gallon cans and would therefore be planted as you would any 1-gallon shrub.

If you are working with a heavy clay soil, don't start with a rotary tiller. You're likely to jar a few teeth loose if you do. First, roughly turn over the soil with a garden fork and then churn it with the rotary tiller. As you dig and till, carefully remove any weeds or grass you encounter, particularly Bermuda grass, nutgrass, and Johnsongrass. If your area is particularly plagued by these pernicious weeds, now is the time to eliminate them. After you till the soil, water it thoroughly and wait for a week or two. This will allow time for the terrible trio to begin to grow and reveal their presence.

Root them out and cast them into a fiery furnace (or a trash can if handier).

Now, add the organic matter and other materials you have selected and thoroughly mix them to a depth of about 6 inches. Smooth the surface of the bed with a garden rake, considering surface drainage as you do, and remove any large clods of dirt remaining on the surface (put these in your compost pile).

Installing an Edger. One frequently overlooked facet of making a groundcover bed is the delineation of its edges with some type of constructed edger. If the edger is wide enough, such as an eight-inch-wide concrete or brick mowing band, it becomes a strong element of the overall design, very clearly outlining the groundcover bed. More

This brick mowing band effectively separates grass and groundcover (Emerald zoysia grass and Dwarf Confederate Jasmine), makes lawn mowing and edging easier, and strongly defines the shape of both grass and groundcover areas.

Edging Materials

There are many groundcover edging materials from which to choose. The one you select depends on your budget, the shape of your groundcover bed, the size of your yard (and therefore its proportional relationship to the width of the edger), and the design effect you desire. Here are the most commonly used and available materials:

Metal

Commercially manufactured metal edgers are available in thicknesses from ⅛-inch to ¼-inch and widths of 4 inches or 5 inches. Metal pegs are usually provided. These slip through slots in the side of the edger for anchoring to the ground. Metal edgers are durable and long-lasting. They are best used for curving shapes but are satisfactory for straight lines if installed carefully.

Plastic

Commercially manufactured plastic edgers are available in thicknesses from ⅛-inch to ¼-inch and widths of about 4 inches to 9 inches. Made of polyethylene or polyvinyl chloride (PVC). Pegs of various types are provided for anchoring. Best for curving shapes, but satisfactory for short straight lines if installed carefully.

Wood

All of the wood edgers are simply standard lumber stock available at local lumber yards. The sizes most often used are 1″ x 4″ and 2″ x 4″, and a special material called bender board, ⅜″ x 4″ (redwood only—you may have to search a little for this one). Construction grade redwood is the most commonly used wood, but southern yellow pine that has been pressure-treated with a wood preservative is just as good and somewhat less expensive. The wood preservative should be of the chromated copper arsenate (CCA) type, marketed under various trade names (Wolman, Osmose K-33, Boliden, Erdalith, Greensalt). This type will not damage plants as will most other wood preservatives used in pressure-treating.

Use 1″ x 4″ boards for "easy" curves of large radius. Bender boards are best for the tighter curves as they are very flexible. Try soaking the boards with water prior to bending. This will make them easier to bend and help reduce breakage. 2″ x 4″ boards are best for straight lines or very slight curves, as they are fairly rigid.

If you have both straight lines and curves as a part of the edge and you want to use a 2″ wide edger, use two 1″ x 4″ boards or five bender boards side by side for the curves. Be sure to stagger the joints on the curved portions so they don't all occur at the same place. Otherwise, you will have created a weak joint that can get out of line if the soil moves about a little bit or if the edger is bumped with something heavy, like a lawn mower.

All boards must be anchored to the ground with wooden stakes. 1″ x 2″ x 12″ or 2″ x 2″ x 12″ stakes, pointed on one end, will work well. Place stakes on alternating sides of the edger at a spacing of about 4 or 5 feet apart, or closer if needed to keep a good smooth line. Drive the stakes into the ground next to the edger and nail them to the side of the edger using galvanized nails.

Various sizes of heavy timbers are also useful as edgers (4″ x 6″, 8″ x 8″, etc.), some pressure treated, some not. Old railroad ties are also frequently used. Timbers can be used in straight lines only. Be careful in using timbers, as they will be a very strong design element, much like concrete or brick mowing bands, and can visually overpower small spaces. The smaller timbers (4″ x 4″, 6″ x 6″) will require anchoring with wood stakes to keep them from floating in heavy rains.

metal edger and pegs

plastic edger with hold-down rods

wood edger with stakes

Almost all edgers must be anchored to the ground to keep them from moving about. Different types of edgers require different devices.

joints staggered for strength

2 × 4 wood edger

two 1 × 4 wood edgers

Curved portions of wood edgers can be made wider by using multiple boards side by side. Pay attention to the location of joints.

common, however, are edgers that are much thinner (⅛ inch up to 2 inches) which are used merely to delineate the edge between groundcover and grass. An edger helps insure that both groundcover and grass are trimmed along the same line every time, thus maintaining the original shape of the bed.

Narrow edgers such as this 2″ × 4″ board, function mostly to delineate the edge between groundcover and grass. Contrast this photo with those on page 46 where no edger was used.

Occasionally, edgers function to keep running types of groundcovers out of lawns, and vice versa. In the South, where our grasses are stoloniferous, both grass and groundcover can freely travel over the edger and must be trimmed periodically.

Edgers should be used in any situation where grass and groundcover meet, unless the design intent is to create a freer, more natural appearance. Obviously, no edger is necessary where a groundcover is adjacent to pavement or a wall.

Except in the case of concrete or brick mowing bands, the technique of installing an edger is roughly the same for all types. Begin by excavating a trench along the edge of the bed to the depth of the edging material and about 3 to 8 inches wide, depending on the material used. Stretch a string line in the exact location of the edger if you are working with straight lines. If the edge is curved, using your "calibrated eyeball" will suffice (just keep the curve flowing smoothly). Set the edger in the trench and secure it to the ground with pegs or stakes. Materials sold specifically as groundcover or flower bed edgers include pegs as a part of the package. Boards or timbers must be anchored with wooden stakes nailed to the side of the edger.

Adjust the level of the top of the edger to be at or slightly above the level of adjacent grass sod (not the tips of the grass blades) if in an established lawn, or about 1 inch to 1½ inches above the soil

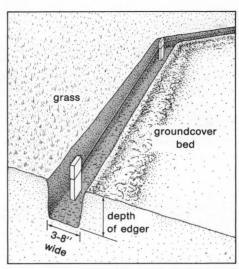

Trenching for the installation of an edger is best accomplished after the groundcover bed is prepared and prior to planting.

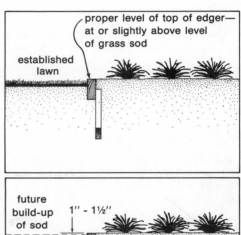

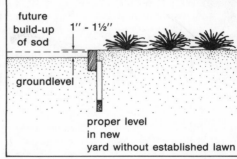

Setting the edger at the proper level is important if it is to function properly.

level in new plantings to allow for build-up of grass sod. The idea here is not to create a mini-retaining wall but to provide a line of demarcation. Where an edger butts into a paved surface, the top of the edger should be set flush with the top of the pavement. This eliminates the possibility of someone tripping over the edger, and it makes a better looking juncture.

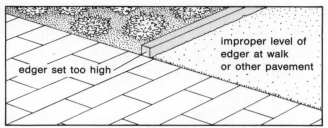

An improper relationship of edger to paving is ugly and can be hazardous to pedestrians.

Soil Preparation on Steep Slopes. Slopes that are approximately 50% or steeper (a 100% slope is a 45° angle) cannot be prepared for planting in the same manner as flat areas. Not only is it physically difficult and dangerous to till the slope, it shouldn't be done. Doing so would only add to your erosion problems because the looser soil would be more erodible. Instead, each plant should have an individually prepared hole.

First, the slope should be covered with an erosion-control netting to minimize surface erosion until the groundcover plants grow enough to cover and bind the soil. Several materials are manufactured for this purpose, including nettings made of jute, shredded wood fibers held together with woven nylon strings, and woven strings made of twisted heavy kraft paper. Generally, the more open weaves are easier to pull weeds through. These nettings are usually sold only by horticultural supply firms. Your local nurseryman, however, can assist you in obtaining them.

Lay the netting on the slope and secure it in place with U-shaped metal pins provided with the netting. At the top of the slope, tuck the netting into a trench and cover it with soil. At each plant location, cut an "X" into the netting and lay back the flaps. You'll find it easier to burn a hole in the nylon types with a rented blow torch. Don't use the torch on the jute or wood fiber types, since they are flammable. Now you are ready to prepare each individual hole for planting.

PLANTING

After the soil has been properly prepared, an edger installed, and the surface of the bed raked smooth and free of clods, you are ready for planting. If you intend to naturalize bulbs in your groundcover bed, now is the time to plant them—before the groundcovers. Check the section on weed control (page 60) to make sure the herbicide you intend to use will not damage bulbs. Now is also the time to plant any trees or shrubs to be included within the bed area.

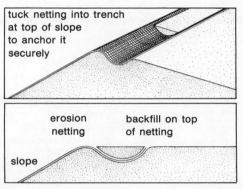

Preparing a slope for erosion control with groundcovers.

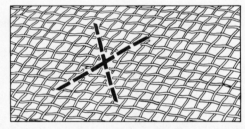

Cut an "X" in erosion netting to facilitate planting.

Lay out the groundcover plants in rows at the recommended spacing (refer to each individual plant in the Encyclopedia on pages 68-86). On slopes, use a staggered spacing to help stop erosion.

For groundcovers being planted in individually prepared holes rather than tilled areas, dig the holes twice as wide as the root ball and half again as deep as the ball. Backfill around the plants with a prepared mixture such as ½ topsoil and ½ organic matter or ⅓ topsoil, ⅓ sand, and ⅓ organic matter. Don't forget to add fertilizer to each hole (follow package instructions).

All groundcover plants, regardless of size, should be set in the ground so that the top of the root ball is just slightly above the top of the soil (to allow for a little settling of soil under the plant). If you have selected the proper groundcover, located and prepared the bed properly, there should be little need to set the top of the root ball very much

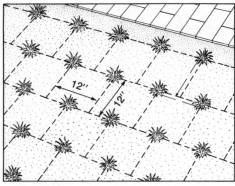

Staggered spacing of groundcover plants is useful on slopes to help control erosion.

Groundcovers in peat pots require special attention in planting. **Left:** Peat pot is planted too high; pot acts as a wick and draws water out of soil. **Right:** Planted at proper depth, water infiltrates roots from soil.

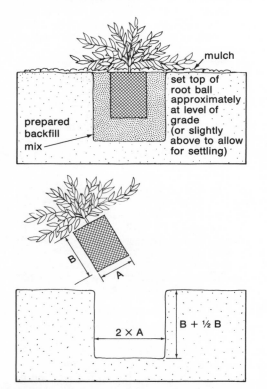

Groundcovers requiring individually prepared holes should be planted in this manner.

above the soil. This practice leads to drying of the exposed portion of the root ball, sometimes even when mulched.

Groundcovers in peat pots are planted pot and all, and must be set so that the pot is entirely covered by the soil. Otherwise, the pot acts as a wick and dries out the root ball.

Balled-and-burlapped plants should have the top ⅓ of the burlap removed after planting. If left on, this portion of the burlap will impede the flow of water into the root ball during the crucial establishment period.

If the herbicide you are using is to be added now, do so and incorporate it into the soil as stated on the package (see section on weed control, page 60).

Don't wait too long to thoroughly water-in the newly planted groundcovers, particularly if they are from flats or small pots. You may need to water a section at a time as you plant to prevent wilting (particularly in the summer or on windy days).

Some groundcovers, particularly the vining types, will benefit from pruning of the tips to make them bushier and produce more runners. This is more easily done prior to planting than after.

Mulching

Mulching is an important horticultural practice with any type of planting, and particularly so with groundcovers. The name of the game is to grow the groundcovers as fast as you can and suppress the weeds for as long as you can. Mulching helps shade out weeds and provides a good growing environment for the roots of the groundcovers.

To be effective, a mulch should be as thick as possible short of smothering the plants. The intent is to provide a cover solid enough to exclude sun from the soil (and therefore inhibit weed growth) but open enough to allow air and water to filter down to the soil. You must gauge the required thickness by the nature of the mulch used, the size of the groundcover plants when planted (the "smother factor"), and the size of your budget. Generally, a thickness of 2 to 4 inches is sufficient.

Usually, a mulch is applied after the groundcovers have been planted. However, with some of the smaller plants, the mulch can be applied first and the groundcovers planted through it. This is easier than trying to place the mulch around and between the small plants. Be sure to plant the

Mulching Materials

As with so many gardening materials, availability of mulches is subject to local variation. If you have a choice, here is some information to help you select one:

Good Choices

Bark. In the South, pine bark is usually readily available and relatively inexpensive. Use the shredded form as it looks the best and doesn't float away as readily as the nuggets (bark chips that are available in various graded sizes). Sometimes pine bark is offered as a "soil conditioner" in a very finely ground form. This is not suitable for mulch, as it tends to be easily blown or washed away. Pine bark is acid in reaction. Add nitrogen to compensate for the amount lost in the decomposition process (see table on page T-2). Redwood and fir bark chips are also available in various sizes, but are usually more expensive than pine bark. Otherwise, they have the same characteristics as pine nuggets. Apply the various barks to a depth of about three inches.

Bagasse (Sugar cane pulp). This has great water-holding capacity (a potential problem for groundcovers susceptible to crown rot). It is acid in reaction and slow to decompose. Apply 1 to 2 inches deep.

Leaves. Obviously not commercially available. Leaves from different species of trees have different characteristics when used as a mulch. Some will pack together and exclude air from the soil. These should be stirred occasionally. Don't use them around vining types of groundcovers, as you are likely to uproot some plants in the process of stirring. Shredded leaves are best for groundcover beds, since they do not pack together as much and fit better around the small plants.

Live Oak leaves are acid in reaction and do not pack down. Other types of oak leaves may pack a little more. Maple and elm leaves are alkaline. Maple and poplar leaves tend to pack together. Non-packing or shredded leaves can be applied 2 to 4 inches deep.

Pine Needles (Pine Straw). Of course, these, too, are leaves. They're acid in reaction, slow to decompose, and allow good air and water penetration. Pine needles don't absorb water themselves; they're better when shredded. Potential fire hazard when dry. Apply about 2 to 4 inches deep.

Wood Chips. Available from local tree service companies, often free (particularly from those trimming trees for utility companies). Slow to decompose, coarse and therefore allowing good air and water penetration. Varying in pH depending on the trees included (usually a mixture and therefore hard to know the composition). Add nitrogen to compensate for the amount lost in decomposition. Apply 2 to 3 inches deep.

These Are Not the Best

Plastic. Used effectively in farming but not really suitable for groundcover beds. In order to allow water to penetrate, holes must be made in the plastic. Weeds come through the holes. When the weeds are pulled, a larger hole is ripped in the plastic, etc., etc., etc. Also, the plastic is very unattractive. If covered with another mulch to improve appearance, the cost gets out of hand. The runners of trailing groundcovers are unable to root in the ground if a plastic mulch is used.

Peat Moss. Good as a soil conditioner (although expensive) but not as good for mulching. It is difficult to wet once it becomes dry, and it tends to cake on the surface, repelling water. Also, when dry, peat moss is flammable and easily blown about by the wind.

Rice Hulls. Another good soil conditioner that does not double as a mulch. The surface dries out rapidly and cakes somewhat. Also, rice hulls are easily blown about by the wind and, being very small, tend to get into a lot of unauthorized places.

Sawdust. The biggest problem with sawdust as a mulch is the fact that it cakes on the surface. When it is loose, it is easily blown by the wind.

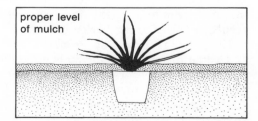

proper level of mulch

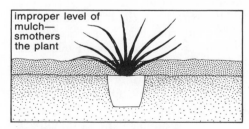

improper level of mulch— smothers the plant

Proper thickness of mulch allows normal development of the plant.

groundcovers in the soil, not in the mulch. This method of mulching is not as effective for groundcovers in large containers because in the process of digging holes some of the mulch is scattered and covered with soil.

In most cases groundcover herbicides and organic mulches don't mix well since the mulch tends to tie-up the herbicide and reduce its effectiveness. A possible solution in some plantings is to apply a short-lived herbicide for control of the initial burst of weeds and then add a mulch just before the herbicide has lost its effectiveness. Another solution is to use a higher application rate of the herbicide. Test the new rate on a small area of groundcover to be sure no damage results.

Care Immediately After Planting

Small groundcover plants are very susceptible to drying and must be watered lightly but frequently for the first few weeks (perhaps every day in the summer). Once they're established and have begun to grow, less frequent but more thorough watering will encourage deep rooting and inhibit germination of weed seeds.

Begin your weed control program now by watching for and eliminating weeds regularly as they appear. Don't let them get out of hand. Replacing the mulch that is scattered by rain and weed removal is an important part of the program.

Weed Control & Groundcover Maintenance

If you were to ask the proud owner of a beautifully grown groundcover bed what his biggest problem was in establishing the groundcover, his smile would probably turn to a frown and he would nastily say "Weeds!" Although weeds are definitely the primary problem to be dealt with in growing groundcovers, don't let them dampen your enthusiasm, for there are solutions.

Total elimination of weeds is not a realistic goal. Rather, strive for *control* of the pesky intruders, because even the most meticulously cared-for groundcover bed will continue to generate new weeds. Of course, once the groundcover has matured and formed a solid cover, the problem is greatly diminished, though still present. Control of weeds is best accomplished through a combination of techniques, all aimed at the goal of replacing weeds with desirable groundcovers as quickly as

possible. The longer the soil remains uncovered, the longer the problem of weeds exists.

NON-CHEMICAL WEED CONTROL

Elimination of Seed Source

A good place to start your weed control program is any place in the yard that weeds are growing. Destroy weeds wherever you find them, particularly before they go to seed—elimination of the seed source will help prevent future problems. Of course, if there are weedy vacant lots or fields nearby that are not under your control, your efforts will be hampered somewhat.

Mulching

Another basic part of weed control is the use of a weed-suppressing mulch. If applied at planting time when all weed growth has been eliminated, and periodically replenished to maintain a solid cover, mulches can help stop some of the weeds before they have a chance to get started. Other weeds will germinate from seeds blown onto the surface of the mulch but are easily removed from the loose mixture.

Replenishing the mulch around certain types of groundcovers, such as vining and running types (particularly very flat growers), is difficult once they have begun to grow together. At this stage of growth, you should concentrate on the use of herbicides and hand-pulling methods. Consult the discussion of mulching on page 32 for further details.

Cultivation

The best and most common method of controlling weeds in most groundcover beds is to pull or hoe them out. There are several things you should bear in mind about this method.

First, don't let the weeds get too large. Removal of large weeds is more difficult, unduly scatters the mulch, and sometimes uproots the groundcovers in the process. Also, large weeds provide stiff competition for moisture and nutrients, with which many groundcovers cannnot cope. Definitely don't allow the weeds to produce seed. A few minutes regularly spent in weed removal will result in better groundcover growth.

The various types of groundcovers must be cultivated differently. Hoeing is effective between shrubby groundcovers if you do it lightly so as to minimize disturbance to feeder roots just under the surface. Hand pulling is best for vining and running types and for shrubby types with branches that root when they touch the ground. Hoeing these groundcovers would uproot too many runners or rooted branches.

CHEMICAL WEED CONTROL—HERBICIDES

A relatively new aspect of the total weed control program for groundcovers is the use of herbicides. Unfortunately, too little is known about the use of herbicides on groundcovers, either by the average gardener or the chemical manufacturers. To date, only limited research has been conducted on the tolerance of specific groundcovers to specific herbicides. Admittedly, the subject is complex. Part of the complexity is that plants used as groundcovers belong to many different families and genera and therefore react differently to herbicides. Also, the environmental and cultural conditions under which groundcovers are grown vary widely, causing a corresponding variance in the effects of herbicides on both groundcovers and weeds.

Too often, chemicals—whether insecticides, fungicides, fertilizers, or herbicides—are seen as an end unto themselves. But herbicides are only one part of a total weed-control program, and they cannot provide 100% elimination of weeds. You must also realize that the benefits of herbicides are accompanied by some risk because of the complexity of the interacting factors involved in their use.

Most herbicide labels list only the generic names of the tolerant groundcovers. This should not be construed to mean that the herbicide can be used on all species and varieties within that genus, although it may be a promising indication. Either test the herbicide on a small portion of the groundcover you have selected or forget about using a herbicide and use a mulch instead.

Herbicide Types

Herbicides are classified in many different ways. For purposes of this discussion, they may be classified into *pre-emergence* and *post-emergence* types. Pre-emergence herbicides are applied to the soil before germination of weed seeds, whereas post-emergence herbicides are applied directly to the weeds after they have appeared. Pre-emergence types are the most useful for groundcovers. When applied at proper rates, these herbicides kill germinating seedlings only and are not effective on weeds beyond the seedling stage.

Although soil fumigants are not technically classified as pre-emergence herbicides, they are used as such; that is, they are applied before the weeds emerge. They are particularly effective in control-ling perennial weeds. Some fumigants (methyl bromide) are very dangerous and require special equipment and techniques for application. These, however, are only available to the professional (see page 43). The types available to the homeowner (Vapam, for example), are not as dangerous and are easier to apply. They are usually applied as a liquid and tilled or washed into the soil and then sealed into the soil by heavy watering. A waiting period of a couple of weeks is necessary before planting (read the label instructions carefully).

Post-emergence herbicides (such as Amitrol) can be used in groundcover beds for spot treatment of hard-to-kill perennial weeds, preferably when the weeds are young. These herbicides must be carefully applied to the weeds only, as most of them will also kill the groundcovers.

Factors Involved in Control with Herbicides

Before you can wisely select a herbicide, you must be aware of the various interacting factors involved in its use. Consider first the *plants* involved. You will, of course, know the groundcover being used, but you should also know which weeds will most likely be encountered, at least the major ones (see pages 32-36 for illustrations of various intrusive weeds and grasses). No herbicide will kill all of the weeds. Most are more or less specific as to the type of weeds on which they have the greatest effect. Some kill mostly grasses, others mostly broadleaved weeds. Still others kill a good selection of each type. Most of the pre-emergence herbicides are not effective against perennial weeds with persistent plant parts such as tubers (nutgrass) or rhizomes (Johnsongrass), although some provide limited control. The soil fumigants are best for these tough ones. A good approach is to select a herbicide that will control the weeds likely to be your biggest pests without damaging the groundcover you intend to plant. The lesser weeds not controlled by the herbicide can then be managed by other means (hoeing, hand pulling, mulching).

If you intend to plant anything other than groundcovers, be doubly careful in your selection of a herbicide. Some will damage bulbs. Most groundcover herbicides, however, are reasonably safe around trees and shrubs planted in the groundcover bed. Those that have a tendency to leach, (the tendency to wash downward into the soil) can cause problems. Always read the label carefully.

Soil type has much to do with the action of a herbicide. Heavy clay soils and soils with a high organic content tend to adsorb, or hold on to, more herbicide than light, sandy soils. The leaching

Herbicides for Your Groundcovers

The herbicides listed here are some of the major ones designed for use in ornamental plantings, including groundcovers. The information given is not comprehensive but is intended as a guide to help you select a herbicide for your situation. Read all instructions and cautions on the label before making your final choice.

Each herbicide is first listed by its common chemical name, with some of its trade names in parentheses. The use of manufacturers' registered trade names is *not* an endorsement and does *not* represent selection by merit of a particular product.

Bensulide (Betasan, Pre San, Prefar)

Controls a selection of annual broadleaved weeds and grasses. Will not damage most well established lawn grasses. Some bulbs are tolerant. Appears to be most effective on alkaline rather than acid soils and on soils low in organic matter. Do not use in conjunction with a mulch. Apply only to well-established groundcovers.

DCPA (Dacthal, Fertilome Weed and Grass Preventer, Oust, Dacthalor)

One of the safest and most readily available in small quantities. Controls a selection of annual broadleaved weeds and grasses. Will not damage most adjacent lawn grasses. Very little leaching (strongly adsorbed). Good for lighter soils. Do not use with a mulch. Apply at planting time and cultivate or water in. Cultivation after application will destroy effectiveness. Controls for two to four months.

Dichlobenil (Casoron)

Controls annual broadleaved weeds and some grasses (better on broadleaved weeds). Controls some perennial weeds in established plantings. Will injure lawn grasses. Low leaching characteristic (but don't use on steep slopes). Not greatly affected by mulches. Best when cultivated in. Not long-lasting.

Diphenamid (Dymid, Enide)

Controls many annual grasses and a few broadleaved weeds. Will injure lawn grasses. Some bulbs are tolerant. May leach in sandy soils; best when incorporated into the soil. May be applied at planting time. Soil can be cultivated after application. Lasts for six to eight months on heavy soils.

EPTC (Eptam)

Perhaps the most commonly available herbicide for ornamentals in the home garden. Available in small quantities. Effectively controls annual grasses and broadleaved weeds. Will control some perennial weeds, specifically nutgrass and quackgrass, at higher application rates (control is good but not complete). Reasonably effective against Bermuda grass. Will damage lawn grasses and bulbs. Best on soils low in organic matter (do not use with a mulch). Must be incorporated into the soil rapidly to prevent breakdown of the chemical. Apply either before or after planting. Has a short life (two to three months) which makes it possible to control initial weeds and then apply a mulch.

Simazine (Princep, Primatol S, CET)

Controls broadleaved weeds and a few annual grasses. Will damage some lawn grasses and not others. Some bulbs are tolerant. Not recommended for sandy soils or steep slopes (will leach). Incorporate into the soil on established plantings. May last for a year or more. When used at high rates of application, Simazine is a soil sterilant.

Trifluralin (Treflan)

Excellent control of annual grasses and many broadleaved weeds. Will damage all lawn grasses but can be used on some bulbs. Organic matter in the soil increases its toxicity (can be used with a mulch). Will not leach (strongly adsorbed). Incorporate into the soil either before or after planting. Can be cultivated lightly after application (no deeper than the treated layer). Lasts for approximately six months. Widely used in California.

HERBICIDE CAUTIONS

* Do not use turf herbicides on groundcovers. Use only those herbicides specifically recommended for use on ornamentals, including groundcovers.
* Be careful in selecting "Weed and Feed" products for use on groundcovers. Many of these contain turf herbicides which will damage groundcovers.
* Do not use herbicides on fruiting groundcovers unless recommended for that specific groundcover. This is important if the plants are grown in an area where someone, particularly children, might unknowingly eat some of the fruit.
* Do not assume that if some is good, more is better. Some groundcover herbicides become total vegetation killers and even soil sterilants at high rates.
* Store herbicides in their original containers, away from children and pets.
* Do not be afraid of herbicides, but do use them wisely.
* Do follow all instructions and heed all warnings printed on the label.

characteristic of some herbicides is, therefore, more pronounced in sandy soils. Groundcovers that are not damaged by a particular herbicide in clay soils may be damaged by the same herbicide in sandy soils. For this reason, application rates are usually lower for sandy soils. Conversely, application rates on clay soils or soils naturally high in organic matter may need to be increased to compensate for the amount of herbicide tied up by the soil. The reverse effect occurs, however, with the herbicide Trifluralin (Treflan), which is made more toxic by the presence of organic matter.

The leaching characteristic of a herbicide becomes an important factor when the herbicide is used on a slope above other plantings, particularly grass (many of the groundcover herbicides are toxic to lawn grasses). In sandy soils particularly, the herbicide may leach down the slope and onto the adjacent plantings with potentially damaging results. Select non-leaching herbicides for such situations.

Pre-emergence herbicides are dependent on *moisture* in the soil to activate and carry them into the top few inches of soil where they can act on germinating weed seeds. Moisture in the air (humidity) also is important in the application of herbicides in spray form. High humidity helps prevent the herbicide from evaporating before it is incorporated into the soil.

Temperature has a definite effect on the action of herbicides. Generally, the higher the temperature, the more effective the herbicide is on weeds, and the more damaging it may be to desirable plants. Poor results often occur in cold weather. Also, ice formation in the surface layers of soil can concentrate a herbicide to the point of damaging the groundcovers.

Sunlight breaks down pre-emergence herbicides and makes them ineffective. For this reason, these herbicides should be incorporated into the soil by watering or cultivating.

The *time of year* that a herbicide is applied has much to do with the degree of control obtained. Although some weeds have seeds germinating pretty much all year round, the majority are fairly seasonal. Herbicide applications should be scheduled to precede the time of germination of the majority of the season's weeds. This means application in late winter to control spring weeds, in spring to control summer weeds, etc. In the milder parts of the South, each season has its own crop of weeds. Therefore, the herbicide must be replenished periodically to maintain control, at least until the groundcover is mature enough to shade out most of the weeds.

Herbicides used by themselves have certain reasonably predictable effects. However, when herbicide mixtures are used the effects are relatively unpredictable. Therefore, unless a particular mixture is specifically recommended, don't use it.

Application Rates

The importance of careful attention to rates of application printed on the label cannot be overstressed. Too high a rate can weaken groundcover plants, slowing their growth and providing more time for the weeds to stage a strong resurgence. Also, some pre-emergence herbicides (Simazine for example), when applied at high rates, become soil sterilants.

If you make a mistake with herbicides, there is a possible solution. There is some evidence, though not totally tested, that the addition of activated charcoal to the soil at a rate of about 4 pounds of active ingredient per 1,000 square feet of area will neutralize some of the herbicide. It's worth a try if you're in this predicament.

MAINTAINING YOUR GROUNDCOVERS

To begin a successful groundcover maintenance program, you must first select the proper plant for your situation. Many failures in gardening are the result of an attempt to force a plant to grow in a situation that is unnatural to it. To be sure, some groundcovers can tolerate a wide variety of environmental conditions, but most are fairly specific in their requirements. Your job of caring for them will be easier if you meet those requirements from the start. The right plant in the right place is more than an ideal—it's a practical necessity for the busy gardener.

The maintenance requirements of groundcovers vary considerably from one species to another. Nevertheless, here are a few general guidelines that will aid you in caring for your plants.

Newly planted groundcovers, even drought-tolerant ones, need frequent watering until they become established. When the plants have settled down and have begun to grow, less frequent but deeper watering (to a depth of at least 6 to 8 inches) will encourage deep root systems that help the plants through periods of hot, dry weather. As with many types of plants, the best time to water groundcovers is early in the day so that the foliage has a chance to dry out before dark. Wet conditions at night foster diseases.

Most groundcovers will benefit from an application of fertilizer at least once a year, preferably in the spring. Those subject to severe root competition under trees may need additional feeding in summer and in early fall. Several light applica-

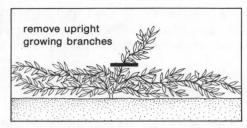

remove upright growing branches

Selective removal of occasional vertical growth, common in some types of groundcovers, maintains desireable low, horizontal habit.

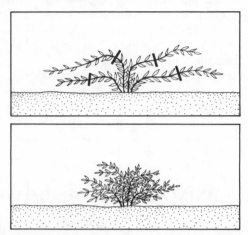

Bushiness must be induced in some groundcovers by trimming. A more solid cover and fewer weeds is the desired result.

tions of granular fertilizers throughout the growing season are better than one heavy dose. The slow-release types are needed less frequently (read package instructions). Apply fertilizers when the foliage is dry; wet leaves can be burned by fertilizer adhering to them.

A certain amount of pruning and trimming is necessary with most groundcovers. Some will require the removal of errant branches, others need occasional pinching or shearing to induce bushiness and promote horizontal growth. Be careful when trimming the tops of the slower-growing ones. If too much top growth is removed, sun can reach the soil and revive dormant weeds before the groundcover can re-grow. Running types will require occasional edging to keep them out of adjacent lawn areas.

The importance of mulches and herbicides in controlling weeds has already been dicussed (see pages 58 to 63). Mulches should be replenished (new mulch added) as needed until the groundcovers have grown enough to make it impossible or unnecessary to add more. For most densely growing groundcovers, application of herbicides can be discontinued when a solid cover of foliage is achieved.

Occasional replanting to replace dead or struggling plants is necessary in most young groundcover beds, particularly if planted from flats or small pots. Replanting may also be necessary in established beds to rejuvenate a portion overcome by perennial weeds. Remove both weeds and groundcovers and start from scratch.

Much has been written in other texts about control of insects and diseases. This is fortunate since space does not allow a complete treatment of the subject in this book (see pages 19-26 for a discussion of insects). Many of the groundcovers listed in the Encyclopedia (pages 68-86) are essentially unencumbered by disease or insect problems. Most of the others are subject only to those pests common to many other ornamentals.

One problem common to areas of the South with heavy soils and humid environments is soil-borne fungus diseases (mostly some form of crown rot or damping-off). The groundcovers themselves often help provide conditions favorable to fungus growth by covering the soil and providing a cool, moist atmosphere at soil level. Soil fungicides such as Captan or Terrachlor (PCNB) usually provide effective control. In many instances, the problem can be prevented by proper selection of a groundcover, provision of a well-drained soil, and careful attention to watering in the early stages of growth.

A Groundcover Selection System

One of the most important aspects of making a groundcover bed is selection of the proper plant (see discussion on page 47). This book includes two features that can help you choose just the right groundcover for your particular situation. The first is a chart called the Groundcover Selection Guide (pages 66-67), and the second is the Encyclopedia of Southern Groundcovers (pages 68-86). When used together, they form a groundcover selection system.

How to Use the System

The Groundcover Selection Guide is intended to be the first step in the selection process. In choosing a groundcover, there are a few major factors that will always strongly govern your choice. These are the ones included in the Guide. Use the Guide to obtain a list of several groundcovers that seem to fulfill your requirements.

Next, refer to the Encyclopedia of Southern Groundcovers for additional information about

Ophiopogon japonicus
(Monkey Grass)

Ilex cornuta 'Rotunda'
(Dwarf Chinese Holly)

Duchesnea indica
(Mock Strawberry)

Hedera helix
(English Ivy)

The Varying Textures of Groundcovers

each plant to help you make your final choice. The Encyclopedia can be used by itself to study a particular plant. The Guide is not intended to be used alone as an information source—the categories are not complete enough for that purpose.

The Groundcover Selection Guide is most efficiently used in the following manner:

1. Place a plain 3 x 5 card on the chart with the longest edge of the card immediately below the column headings.

2. On the card, mark with a dot or an arrow the columns that are of importance to you.

3. As you slide the card down the page, keeping the marks lined up with the appropriate columns, you can quickly find the plants that fit all or some of your requirements. A dot in a column indicates that the plant listed has that characteristic or will grow in that situation. A "V" or an "S" in a column means that a variety (V) of the plant listed, or another species (S) of the same genus has different characteristics than the plant listed and fits the category indicated. The numbers in the "Seashore Conditions" column indicate that the plant listed will tolerate the conditions in the seashore belt of exposure indicated (see explanation below).

The Plants Included In The System

The groundcovers included in this system are the major ones used in the South together with some lesser known but equally useful ones. Not all of the plants listed will grow in your climate. Among the list, however, can be found groundcovers for all parts of the South, from the warmest sub-tropical areas of the lower South (zones 9 and 10) to the colder, more northern-like climates of the upper South (zone 7). Many of the groundcovers whose southerly limit of easy culture is zone 7 are not listed simply for lack of space. Information about these can be found in groundcover books written for northern climates.

Explanation of Column Headings

Many of the column headings in the Guide are self-explanatory. A few, however, require a brief discussion.

Temperature Zones (7-10). These zones correspond to those on the Plant Hardiness Zone Map on page iv and are the only zones included in the area of coverage of this book. Each zone includes within it many micro-climatic areas not typical of the general zone characteristics (either colder or warmer). These zones, however, serve as good general indications of cold hardiness.

Seashore Conditions. The numbers found in this column refer to differing belts of exposure to seashore conditions.

Belt 1 conditions are the most severe. Plants listed for this belt will tolerate salt in the soil and in the air (salt spray), and constantly windy conditions with occasional wind blown sand. These plants will withstand the full fury of a storm and most will endure contact with seawater.

Belt 2 conditions exist behind the protection of a natural or artificial barrier (fence, hedge of Belt 1 plants, etc.). Plants listed for this belt will tolerate salt in the soil and some in the air, but cannot withstand strong winds. Most of these plants cannot tolerate contact with seawater.

Belt 3 conditions are considerably milder than those of Belts 1 and 2. These plants will tolerate a little salt in the soil but none of the rigorous conditions of Belts 1 and 2. Small amounts of salt are still in the air in this belt but if regularly washed off the plants, no damage results. We have been conservative with this list: probably, more plants will tolerate these conditions than are listed.

The information in this column is, for the most part, taken from Edwin Menninger's *Seaside Plants of the World: A Guide to Planning, Planting, and Maintaining Salt-Resistant Gardens*, Hearthside Press Inc., New York, 1964. Readers are referred to this book for an in-depth discussion of seashore gardening.

Narrow Spaces. Plants listed in this category are suitable for growing in narrow planting spaces 3 or 4 feet wide. They can easily be contained and are of small enough proportions that they will not visually overpower the intended space. These are the first plants you should consider for confined areas such as townhouse gardens.

Groundcover Selection Guide

Plant	Height & Growth Rate					Temp.				Light			Soil & Moisture							Uses				
	Under 6"	6-12"	12-18"	Taller than 18"	Fast-growing	Zone 7	Zone 8	Zone 9	Zone 10	Sun	Partial Shade	Full Shade	Acid	Alkaline	Sandy	Clay	Poor	Dry	Wet	Seashore Conditions	Narrow Spaces	Stepping Stones	Steep Slopes	Cascading
Abelia x grandiflora 'Prostrata' (Prostrate Glossy Abelia)			●		●	●	●	●	●	●	●		●	●	●	●				2				●
Achillea tomentosa (Woolly Yarrow)	●	V			●	●	●	●	●	●	●		●	●	●	●	●	●		3	●	●		
Ajuga reptans (Ajuga)	●	V			●	●	●	●		●	●	●	●	●	●						●	●		
Anthemis nobilis (English Camomile)	●				●	●	●	●	●	●	●		●	●	●	●					●	●		
Arctostaphylos uva-ursi (Bearberry)		●	S	S	S	●	●	●	●	●	●		●				●	●		1	●		●	●
Arctotheca calendula (Arctotheca)		●			●		●	●	●	●	●			●	●	●					●		●	
Armeria maritima (Sea-Pink)	●					●	●			●			●	●	●					1	●			
Asparagus sprengeri (Sprenger Asparagus)			●					●	●	●	●		●	●	●					2				●
Baccharis pilularis (Dwarf Coyote Brush)			●	●	●		●	●	●	●	●		●	●	●	●	●	●		1			●	●
Campanula elatines garganica	●		●		●	●	●	●		●	●		●	●		●					●			
Campanula poscharskyana (Serbian Bellflower)		●			●	●	●	●		●	●		●	●							●			
Carissa grandiflora varieties (Natal Plum)		●	●				●	●	●	●	●		●	●	●	●				1				●
Cerastium tomentosum (Snow-in-Summer)	●				●	●	●	●	●	●			●	●	●			●		2	●			
Ceratostigma plumbaginoides (Blue Leadwort)		●			●	●	●	●	●	●	●		●	●	●					2	●			
Coreopsis auriculata 'Nana' (Dwarf Coreopsis)	●				●	●	●	●	●	●	●		●	●				●			●	●		
Cotoneaster species (Cotoneaster)	●	●	●		●	●	●	●		●			●	●	●		●	●		2			●	●
Cyrtomium falcatum (Holly Fern)			●					●	●		●	●	●	●	●					3	●			
Dichondra repens (Dichondra)	●				●		●	●	●	●	●		●	●						3	●	●		
Duchesnea indica (Mock Strawberry)	●	●			●	●	●	●	●	●	●		●	●							●			
Euonymus fortunei (Wintercreeper)	V	V	V		●	●	●	●		●	●	●	●	●	●	●	●	●		1	V	V	●	●
Festuca ovina 'Glauca' (Blue Fescue)		●				●	●	●	●	●	●		●	●	●		●	●		2	●			
Fragaria varieties (Strawberry)		●			●	●	●	●	●	●	●		●	●							●			
Fragaria chiloensis (Sand Strawberry)		●			●	●	●	●	●	●	●		●	●						1	●			
Gardenia jasminoides 'Radicans' (Dwarf Gardenia)			●				●	●	●	●	●		●								●			
Gelsemium sempervirens (Carolina Jessamine)				●	●	●	●	●		●	●		●	●										●
Hedera helix (English Ivy)		●			●	●	●	●			●	●	●	●	●					2	●	V	●	●
Hedera canariensis (Algerian Ivy)		●			●		●	●	●	●	●	●	●	●	●				●	1			●	●
Heuchera sanguinea (Coral Bells)		●				●	●	●	●	●	●		●	●						2	●			
Hypericum calycinum (Dwarf Hypericum)		●			●	●	●	●	●	●	●		●	●	●						●		●	
Iberis sempervirens (Evergreen Candytuft)	V	●			●	●	●	●	●	●	●		●	●						2	●		●	
Ilex species (Holly)		●	●			●	●	●	●	●	●		●	●						2	●			
Juniperus chinensis sargentii (Sargent Juniper)		●				●	●	●	●	●			●	●	●					2			●	●
Juniperus conferta (Shore Juniper)		●	●			●	●	●		●			●	●	●					1			●	●
Juniperus horizontalis (Prostrate Juniper)	V	V	●			●	●	●	●	●			●	●	●	●				2			●	●
Juniperus procumbens (Japanese Garden Juniper)		V		●		●	●	●	●	●			●	●						2			●	●
Juniperus sabina 'Tamariscifolia' (Tam Juniper)			V	●		●	●	●	●	●			●	●	●					2			●	●
Juniperus virginiana 'Silver Spreader'			●			●	●	●	●	●			●	●									●	●
Liriope muscari (Liriope)		●				●	●	●	●	●	●		●	●	●					3	●			
Liriope spicata (Creeping Lily-Turf)	●					●	●	●	●	●	●		●	●	●					2	●			
Lonicera japonica 'Halliana' (Hall's Honeysuckle)			●	●	●	●	●	●		●	●		●	●	●	●	●		●	2			●	●

Groundcover Selection Guide

Plant	Under 6"	6-12"	12-18"	Taller than 18"	Fast-growing	Zone 7	Zone 8	Zone 9	Zone 10	Sun	Partial Shade	Full Shade	Acid	Alkaline	Sandy	Clay	Poor	Dry	Wet	Seashore Conditions	Narrow Spaces	Stepping Stones	Steep Slopes	Cascading
Height & Growth Rate spans Under 6"–Fast-growing; **Temp.** spans Zone 7–Zone 10; **Light** spans Sun–Full Shade; **Soil & Moisture** spans Acid–Wet; **Uses** spans Seashore Conditions–Cascading																								
Lysimachia nummularia (Moneywort)	•			•	•	•	•	•			•	•	•								•	•		•
Malephora crocea (Croceum Iceplant)		•		•			•	•	•	•			•	•	•		•	•		1	•		•	
Malephora luteola (Yellow Trailing Iceplant)		•		•			•	•		•			•	•	•		•	•		1	•			
Nepeta hederacea (Ground Ivy)	•			•	•	•	•	•	•		•	•	•	•	•	•				3	•	•		
Ophiopogon japonicus (Monkey Grass)		•			•	•	•	•	•	•	•	•	•	•						2	•			
Pachysandra terminalis (Pachysandra)		•			•	•	•	•	•		•	•	•	•						2	•		•	
Paxistima canbyi (Canby Paxistima)		•			•	•	•	•		•	•		•								•			
Phlox subulata (Moss-Pink)		•		•		•	•	•	•	•			•	•			•	•			•			•
Pittosporum tobira 'Wheelers Dwarf' (Wheeler's Dwarf Pittosporum)			•			•	•	•	•	•	•		•	•						1				
Polygonum capitatum (Pinkhead Knotweed)		•		•			•	•	•	•			•		•	•					•			
Potentilla crantzii (Spring Cinquefoil)	S	•		•		•	•	•	•	•	•		•	•	•	•		S			•	•		
Pyracantha koidzumi 'Santa Cruz' (Santa Cruz Pyracantha)			•			•	•	•		•			•	•			•	•		3				
Ranunculus repens (Creeping Buttercup)		•		•		•	•	•	•		•	•	•						•		•			
Rosmarinus officinalis 'Prostratus' (Dwarf Rosemary)		•	•			•	•	•		•			•	•	•	•	•	•		1	•		•	•
Santolina chamaecyparissus (Gray Santolina)			•			•	•	•	•	•			•	•	•	•	•	•		1	•		•	•
Santolina virens (Green Santolina)		•		•		•	•	•	•	•			•	•	•	•	•	•		1	•		•	•
Sarcococca hookeriana humilis (Sweet Box)		•	•			•	•				•	•	•								•			
Sasa pygmaea (Dwarf Bamboo)		•		•		•	•	•	•		•	•	•	•					•		•		•	
Saxifraga stolonifera (Strawberry Begonia)	•					•	•	•	•		•	•	•	•							•			
Sedum acre (Goldmoss Stonecrop)	•			•		•	•	•	•	•			•	•	•	•	•	•		2	•	•		
Sedum album (White Stonecrop)	•			•		•	•	•	•	•			•	•	•	•	•	•		1	•	•		
Sedum anglicum (English Stonecrop)	•			•		•	•	•	•	•			•	•	•	•	•	•		2	•	•		
Sedum confusum		•		•		•	•	•	•	•			•	•	•	•	•	•		2	•			•
Sedum dasyphyllum (Gray Stonecrop)	•			•		•	•	•	•	•			•	•	•	•	•	•		2	•			
Sedum lineare (Stringy Stonecrop)		•		•		•	•	•	•	•			•	•	•	•	•	•		2	•			•
Sedum rubrotinctum (Brown Bean Stonecrop)		•		•		•	•	•	•	•			•	•	•	•	•	•		2	•			
Sedum rupestre	•	•		•		•	•	•	•	•			•	•	•	•	•	•		2	•			
Sedum spurium (Two-Row Stonecrop)	V	•		•		•	•	•	•	•			•	•	•	•	•	•		2	•	V		
Senecio cineraria (Dusty Miller)			•	•		•	•	•		•			•	•	•	•	•	•		1				
Thymus serphyllum (Mother-of-Thyme)	•			•		•	•	•	•	•			•	•	•	•	•	•		2	•	•		•
Trachelospermum asiaticum (Japanese Star-jasmine)		•	•			•	•	•	•	•	•		•	•						1				•
Trachelospermum jasminoides (Confederate Jasmine)			•				•	•	•	•	•		•	•						1				•
Trachelospermum jasminoides pubescens (Dwarf Confederate Jasmine)			•				•	•	•	•	•		•	•						1	•			•
Verbena peruviana (Peruvian Verbena)	•	V		•			•	•	•	•			•	•	•	•	•				•			
Vinca major (Bigleaf Periwinkle)			•			•	•	•	•	•	•	•	•	•						3			•	•
Vinca minor (Dwarf Periwinkle)		•				•	•	•			•	•	•	•									•	•
Viola odorata (Sweet Violet)		•		•		•	•	•	•		•	•	•	•									•	
Viola hederacea (Australian Violet)	•			•			•	•			•	•	•	•							•			
Wedelia trilobata (Wedelia)		•		•			•	•	•	•	•		•	•					•	2				•
Zoysia tenuifolia (Korean Grass)	•						•	•	•	•	•		•	•								•	•	

An Encyclopedia of Southern Groundcovers

All plants in the Encyclopedia are listed alphabetically by their currently correct botanical name, with commonly used but incorrect botanical names listed in parentheses. Immediately below the botanical name is the common name most familiar to the author, with other common names in parentheses. The index can be used as a cross-reference to look up a plant by its common name first.

Directly across from the botanical name is the height and, in some cases, the spread of the plant. For plants having a randomly spreading growth habit, only the height is given. In a few instances, spread data were unavailable. This information is followed by the most northerly cold hardiness zone the plant will tolerate (see map on page 55). These zonal indications do not appear to correspond to those on the Groundcover Selection Guide. The listing here is given to indicate the degree of cold the plant will tolerate. The listing on the Guide (zones 7-10) indicates only whether the plant listed will or will not grow in your particular southern zone, and does not indicate its most northerly limit of cold hardiness.

Plants said to be tolerant of environmental stress are those which can withstand the urban conditions of air pollution, general abuse of pedestrians, animals, and sometimes automobiles, and minimum maintenance. The information for this listing is adapted from the American Horticultural Society's *Environmentally Tolerant Trees, Shrubs and Groundcovers*.

The resistance of a plant to the browsing of deer depends on many variables. For example, with an adequate natural food supply, resistant plants probably will be untouched, whereas if a shortage of natural food exists, very few plants are totally resistant to deer. Other factors are also involved, but it is sufficient to say that the plants noted as deer-resistant are probably some of your best choices if you have a deer problem. The information for this listing was obtained from *Deer Resistant Plants For Ornamental Use* by Maynard W. Cummings, Marston H. Kimball, and William M. Longhurst, California Agricultural Experiment Station Extension Service leaflet #167, 1963.

Abelia x grandiflora 'Prostrata' 1½-2' x 5'
Prostrate Glossy Abelia **Zone 6**

Evergreen to semi-deciduous (even in mild climates) woody shrub of the Honeysuckle family (Caprifoliaceae).

Characteristics. Spreading, mounding habit of medium density and moderate growth rate. Leaves dark green with bronzy tints (more pronounced in winter), glossy, ½ - 1" long, oval, pointed. New growth bronzy. Flowers pinkish-white to white, trumpet-shaped, ½ - ¾" long in clusters at the ends of branches, lightly fragrant, not showy from a distance but good up close, summer and early fall.

Culture. Grows in most soils; prefers a fertile, well-drained soil with plenty of organic matter. Likes a regular supply of water. Best growth and flowering is in full sun but will tolerate partial shade. Tolerates Belt 2 seashore conditions. No significant insect or disease problems. Plant 18" to 3' apart.
Herbicides: Bensulide, DCPA (both listed for genus).

Remarks. Best used alone or with an interplanting of trees or large shrubs. Good for cascading over a wall. Not commonly used, but available from California growers in pots or 1-gallon cans (best from cans).

Achillea tomentosa 3-4"
Woolly Yarrow **Zone 3**

Evergreen herbaceous perennial from Europe and Asia. Daisy family (Compositae).

Characteristics. Creeping stems forming a flat mat. Fast-growing. Fern-like, woolly, light olive-green leaves very finely dissected, 2-5" long, aromatic when crushed. Flowers bright golden yellow, individually small, but in showy, flat-topped clusters on 6-10" stems.

Culture. Grows in most well-drained soils, tolerates poor soil. Drought-and-heat-resistant but is best with regular watering in hot months (particularly in the warmer zones). Full sun is best; tolerates light shade. Belt 3 seashore. Plant 6-12" apart. Can be mown infrequently to 2" or sheared to maintain flatness. Remove faded flowers for prolonged bloom. May need thinning if crowded.
Herbicide: Trifluralin (listed for genus).

Remarks. A small-scale plant for small areas, narrow spaces, even between stepping stones if clipped occasionally. Allows bulbs to grow through. Available in flats and probably in pots.

Varieties. A.t. aurea; A.t. 'Moonlight' (1" high, lighter yellow flowers, greener leaves, slower-growing); A.t. nana (white flowers)

Ajuga reptans 2-4"
Ajuga (Carpet Bugle, Bugleweed) **Zone 3**

Evergreen herbaceous perennial from Europe. Mint family (Labiatae)

Characteristics. A flat rosette of leaves from which runners creep on top of or slightly under the soil, rooting as they go, forming a dense flat mat. Fast-growing; can be invasive. Moderately dark green, 4" to 5" long, spoon-shaped leaves develop reddish tones in winter, leaves larger in shade than sun. Blue to purplish-blue flowers appear on short, rigid upright spikes from spring to early summer; showy.

Culture. Prefers a well-drained, fertile, slightly acid to neutral soil, tolerates slightly alkaline and heavy clay soils. Requires constant water supply (not wet), particularly in very hot weather. Partial shade (best) to full shade, colored-leaved varieties color best with more sun. Plant 12" apart. Trim or mow off old flower spikes, feed regularly; requires regular edge trimming. Susceptible to root knot nematodes, fungal diseases (in wet soils).

Herbicides: Bensulide (listed for genus), Diphenamid (possible slight injury with quick recovery), EPTC (listed for genus, possible injury), Trifluralin (slight injury with quick recovery). *Do not use:* DCPA, Simazine.

Remarks. Best used in relatively small areas, good between stepping stones, in narrow spaces; tolerates occasional light traffic. Bulb cover. Tolerates environmental stress; deer-resistant. Very commonly used and available in flats, pots, cans, or from neighbors.

Varieties. A.r. alba (white flowers); A.r. 'Atropurpurea' (Bronze Ajuga, the most common variety, dark bronzy-purple leaves); A.r. 'Rubra' (dark purple leaves); A.r. 'Variegata' (creamy yellow variegation); A.r. 'Metallica Crispa' (curly, metallic leaves); A.r. 'Giant Bronze' (6" to 9" height, bronze leaves); A.r. 'Giant Green' (6" to 9" height, bright green leaves); A.r. 'Jungle Bronze' (leaves large, rounded, 6" height, bronze, clumps); A.r. 'Jungle Green' (largest leaves, rounded, crisp edge, green).

Anthemis nobilis 3-6"
English Chamomile (Roman Camomile) **Zone 5**

Evergreen herbaceous perennial from Europe. Daisy family (Compositae).

Characteristics. Creeping, rooting stems grow moderately fast to form a flat mat. Fern-like, very finely cut leaves are light bright green and aromatic when crushed. Button-like yellow flowers to 12" high produce a pleasing show in summer (some forms have daisy-like flowers, white petals, yellow center).

Culture. Tolerant of most soils. Best with plenty of moisture (not soggy) but will tolerate some dryness. Full sun to very light shade. Plant 6" to 12" apart. Can be mown high or sheared to produce a flatter mat.

Remarks. Useful in small areas, narrow spaces, and between stepping stones. Tolerates some traffic and is used in Europe as a lawn substitute. Good bulb cover, and also useful in the herb garden. Available in flats and pots.

Varieties. A.n. 'Flore-pleno' (double flowers); A.n. 'Grandiflora' (yellow, daisy-like flowers and button-like flowers).

Arctostaphylos uva-ursi 6-12" x 10-15'
Bearberry (Kinnikinnick,
Creeping Manzanita) **Zone 2**

Evergreen woody shrub native to much of the United States from coast to coast and also Mexico. Heath family (Ericaceae).

Characteristics. Prostrate, trailing stems root as they grow flat on the ground. Slow to start, but grows at a moderate rate when established. Leaves are ½" to 1" long, oval, tough and leathery, closely set on branches, bright glossy green, turning bronzy-red in fall. Small (¼") waxy, white or pinkish, bell- or urn-shaped flowers cluster at branch tips in late winter to spring; showy. Tiny apple-like, scarlet to pinkish-red fruits are very showy and loved by birds. Twigs and branches are smooth, dark red to reddish-brown.

Culture. Soil must be very well-drained and acid (pH 5.0). Grows in poor, sandy, rocky soils, but will tolerate heavier soils with sharp drainage. Drought-resistant but needs frequent watering while being established to aid rooting of branches, water sparingly in summer. Best in full, hot sun (too much heat may sometimes brown leaf tips), tolerates light shade. Belt 1 seashore—right on the beach. Plant 3' apart. Clip and pinch tips frequently for bushiness.

Herbicides: Dichlobenil.

Remarks. Covers large areas, can be kept in relatively small areas and narrow spaces by trimming. Good for steep slopes, beach planting, cascading over a wall. Tolerates environmental stress. Difficult to transplant once in the ground. Best planted from 1-gallon cans.

Varieties and Other Species. A.u. 'Point Reyes' (dark green leaves); A.u. 'Radiant' (lighter green leaves, more fruit); A. densiflora 'Harmony' (2-3' x 8-10'); A. densiflora 'Howard McMinn' (2' x 6-8', rose-pink flowers); A. hookeri 'Monterey Carpet' (12" x 12', prostrate); A. hookeri 'Wayside' (30" x 12', vigorous); A. franciscana (6" high, rapid growth).

Arctotheca calendula 8-10"
Arctotheca (Cape Weed, Cape
Gold) **Zones 9-10**

Evergreen (tender) herbaceous perennial from South Africa. A natural bigeneric hybrid between Arctotis and Dimorphotheca. Daisy family (Compositae).

Characteristics. Rosettes of coarse foliage, spreading by thick surface runners that root and produce a plant at each node, forming a low mat of growth. Very fast growth, can easily be invasive. Large, hairy leaves 6" to 8" long, are coarsely and deeply lobed, light gray-olive-green above, silvery beneath. Flowers are bright yellow, daisy-like, 2" across, showy masses in the spring and scattered in the summer.

Culture. Well-drained soil, tolerates heavy clay, rocky, or sandy soil. Somewhat drought-resistant, needs regular watering when young, best with regular watering when established. Full sun or light shade, blooms best in sun. Plant 12" to 18" apart. Requires regular edging, remove old flowers. Crown rot can be a problem in wet soils.

Herbicides: EPTC.

Remarks. Suitable for large areas, can be maintained in smaller areas, narrow spaces, steep slopes (frost-free areas). The old leaves freeze at about 28°, but the crown is undamaged at about 18° and probably lower. Regrowth occurs within a few weeks if freezing weather is not constant. Successfully grown in Houston, Texas. Tolerates environmental stress. Available in flats from California growers.

Armeria maritima (A. vulgaris)   3-6″ x 12″
Sea-Pink (Common Thrift)   **Zone 2**

Evergreen herbaceous perennial from southern Greenland, Iceland, and northwestern Europe. Plumbago family (Plumbaginaceae).

Characteristics. Tufted, cushion-like dense mounds. Moderate growth rate. Finely textured, medium yellow-green, grass-like linear foliage, ⅛″ wide. Flowers are rose-pink, ½-¾″ ball-like heads, very showy in spring and intermittent throughout the year.

Culture. Requires very well-drained soil, light and sandy or rocky soil. Tolerates some dryness except in hottest sun. Full sun (cooler parts of the South) to light shade. Belt 1 seashore. Plant 6″ to 12″ apart. Clip off old flowers for tidiness, feed regularly, thin if too crowded (may die out in center of plant, leaving a hole).

Remarks. For small areas only; narrow spaces, beach gardens, rocky outcroppings. Best in cooler parts of South. Available in flats or pots, possibly 1-gallon cans.

Varieties. A.m. alba (white flowers), A.m. laucheana (deep crimson flowers), other varieties also available.

Asparagus sprengeri   18-24″ x 3-4′
Sprenger Asparagus (Sprenger Fern,
*   Asparagus Fern)*   **Zones 9-10**

Evergreen (tender) semi-woody perennial vine or sub-shrub from South Africa. Lily family (Liliaceae).

Characteristics. Clumps of arching stems form a mounding, tangled growth mass. Stems do not root when they touch the ground. Moderate to fast rate of growth. Leaves are needle-like, 1″ long, light to medium yellow-green (darker in shade). Small (¼″) lightly fragrant, pinkish-white flowers cluster along the stems in summer; not showy from a distance. Winter brings bright red, ¼″ round berries scattered along stems. Stems have a few prickles.

Culture. Grows in most well-drained soils; prefers fertile soil with plenty of organic matter. Drought-resistant but more luxurious with plenty of water. Full sun to light shade (leaves turn yellow in dense shade or hot sun without water). Belt 2 seashore. Plant 12″ to 24″ apart. Its moderate foliage density will allow some weeds. Weeding of established plantings is difficult because of the prickles.
Herbicides: EPTC.

Remarks. Good for cascading over a wall, traffic barrier (because of prickles), small areas. Will climb into shrubs but not trees. Keep away from circulation areas as prickles will catch on clothing. Foliage and stems are killed below about 28° but re-growth occurs from the base in the spring in mild areas. Available in flats, pots and 1-gallon cans.

Varieties. A.s. 'Compacta' (A. sarmentosus), denser, more compact growth.

Baccharis pilularis   12-24″ x 4-6′
Dwarf Coyote Brush (Dwarf
*   Chaparral Broom)*   **Zone 8**

Evergreen woody shrub native to the Oregon and California coast. Daisy family (Compositae).

Characteristics. A spreading, somewhat mounding, dense mass of growth. Fast-growing. Holly-like leaves are olive-green, ½-1″ long, toothed. Flowers are insignificant, male and female on different plants, male form is the one usually sold (female form has messy cottony seeds).

Culture. Almost any soil, sand to clay, well-drained or poorly drained, acid or alkaline. Drought-resistant, but tolerates wet soil and anything in between. Full sun. Belt 1 seashore. Plant 2-3′ apart. Prune out old branches that arch upward, may need thinning to rejuvenate.
Herbicides: DCPA, Diphenamid, Trifluralin, Dichlobenil (partial injury).

Remarks. Excellent for dry slopes, erosion control (deep-rooted), beach plantings, large areas or relatively small areas, cascading over a wall. Available in flats, pots or 1-gallon cans.

Varieties. B.p. 'Twin Peaks'—more compact, lower-growing (to 18″), bright green leaves, plant 18″ to 2′ apart.

Campanula
Bellflower

Evergreen herbaceous perennials of the Bellflower family (Campanulaceae).

Characteristics. See individual species listing.

Culture. Need well-drained, sandy or gravelly soil, tolerate poor soil, best with some fertility and slight alkalinity. Tolerate some dryness; best with regular water supply. Full sun in cool climates, partial shade in hot climates. Plant 6″ to 12″ apart. Snails and slugs can be a problem.
Herbicides: Bensulide (listed for genus).

Remarks. Use for small areas, narrow spaces, or as a bulb cover. Available in flats, pots, 1-gallon cans. Both varieties may lose some leaves in winter in coldest areas.

C. elatines garganica   3-6″ x 10″
**   (C. garganica)**   **Zones 5-6**

Native to Italy. Tufted, with creeping stems. Dense, fast growth. Small, heart-shaped, hairy, toothed leaves are gray-green. Flowers are star-shaped, flat, ½″ across, violet-blue, summer and fall.

C. poscharskyana   6-10″ x 18-24″
Serbian Bellflower   **Zone 4**

Native to Yugoslavia. Tufted, spreading by underground stems forming a dense mass of growth. Fast-growing. Leaves are heart-shaped, toothed, 1″ to 3″ long and wide, slightly hairy. Star-like, ½″-1″ lavender-blue flowers, profuse in spring and summer. Best of the Bellflowers for groundcover.

Carissa grandiflora varieties (C. macrocarpa)
Natal Plum   **Zones 9-10**

Evergreen (tender) woody shrubs. C. grandiflora is from South Africa. Dogbane family (Apocynaceae).

Characteristics. Spreading, mounding growth. Slow to start, moderate growth rate once established. Dark green, shiny, roundish leaves develop reddish tinges in winter, 1″ to 2″ long, depending on variety. Flowers are pure white pin-wheels, 1-2″ wide, very fragrant, borne sporadically throughout the year followed by red, plum-like, edible fruits. Branches and ends of twigs are spiny.

Culture. Grow in any well-drained soil. Tolerate some dryness; best with regular supply of water; do not overwater in clay soils. Full sun to partial shade, bloom best in sun. Belt 1 seashore. Plant 18″ to 24″ apart. Prune out upright stems, weeding is difficult in established plantings because of thorns. Scale insects sometimes a problem.

Remarks. Good for beach plantings, cascading over a wall, relatively small areas or large areas (zone 10). Plant from 1-gallon cans. Plant only in protected or coastal areas in zone 9; best in zone 10.

Varieties. C.g. 'Boxwood Beauty' (dense, mounding, compact, 2′ x 2′, slow-growing, thornless, plant 12″ apart); C.g. 'Green Carpet' (one of the best for ground-cover, 1-1½′ x 4′); C.g. 'Horizontalis' (1½′ x 2′, dense, spreading); C.g. 'Prostrata' (2′, spreading); C.g. 'Tuttle' (2-3′ x 3-5′, dense and compact, heavier flower and fruit production); C.g. 'Tomlinson' (2-2½′ x 3′, compact, slow-growing, thornless, reddish tint to leaves, plant 18″ apart).

Cerastium tomentosum   3-6″ x 2-4′
Snow-in-Summer   **Zone 3**

Evergreen herbaceous perennial from Europe. Pink or Carnation family (Caryophyllaceae).

Characteristics. Wide-spreading by creeping stems forming a low, dense mass of growth. Fast-growing. Leaves are silvery-green, woolly, ¾″ long, ⅛″ wide. White ½″ flowers produce a good show in late spring and summer; self-sowing.

Culture. Requires very well-drained, sandy (even pure sand), poor soil (too much fertilizer causes rank growth), tolerates acid or alkaline soil. Drought-tolerant, best with regular water supply. Full sun to partial shade. Belt 2 seashore. Plant 12″ to 18″ apart. Trim once a year after flowering for bushiness and neatness.
Herbicides: DCPA, Diphenamid, Trifluralin. *Do not use:* Dichlobenil.

Remarks. Best for small areas (not long-lived, perhaps 3 or 4 years), narrow spaces, rocky areas, bulb cover, cascading over a wall. Looks good interplanted with Festuca ovina 'Glauca'. Tolerates some traffic. Looks a little ragged in winter. Available in flats, pots, and perhaps in 1-gallon cans.

Ceratostigma plumbaginoides
(Plumbago larpentae)   6-12″
Blue Leadwort (Dwarf Plumbago)   **Zone 6**

Evergreen to semi-evergreen (in colder areas) perennial from China. Plumbago family (Plumbaginaceae).

Characteristics. Tufted, spreading by underground stems; above-ground stems are thin and wiry. Fast-growing. Medium to dark green, 3″ oval leaves develop bronzy tones in cold weather. Flowers are phlox-like, ¾″ in showy clusters at tips of new growth, deep intense blue to purplish-blue, mid-summer to frost.

Culture. Grows in any well-drained soil, prefers organic matter in soil. Regular supply of water. Sun to partial shade. Belt 2 seashore. Plant 12″ to 18″ apart. Benefits from shearing in spring before new growth starts to remove shabbiness of winter and produce fresh growth for blooming; replace old deteriorated plants.

Remarks. Best for small areas, narrow spaces, bulb cover. A little shabby looking for a short time in winter (more so in colder areas). Available in pots and 1-gallon cans.

Coreopsis auriculata 'Nana'   6″ x 15-18″
Dwarf Coreopsis (Dwarf Eared
*   Coreopsis)*   **Zone 5**

Evergreen to semi-evergreen herbaceous perennial. C. auriculata is native from Virginia to Florida. Daisy family (Compositae).

Characteristics. Rosette of foliage sending out runners to form a flat mat. Fast-growing. Dark green, 2-5″ long leaves. Daisy-like flowers are 2″ across, bright orange-yellow in spring through fall; showy.

Culture. Grows in any soil; best in lighter soils. Drought- and heat-tolerant; best with occasional watering. Full sun to partial shade. Plant 6″ to 12″ apart. Shear off faded flowers.

Remarks. Best used in small areas, narrow spaces, bulb cover, between stepping stones. Available in flats, pots, and 1-gallon cans.

Cotoneaster
Cotoneaster

Evergreen or deciduous woody shrubs. Rose family (Rosaceae).

Characteristics. All species and varieties listed have small white flowers in spring followed by showy red berries. See individual species listing.

Culture. Grow in most well-drained soils; best if slightly alkaline; tolerate poor soil. Drought- and heat-tolerant. Full sun to light shade. Belt 2 seashore (possibly Belt 1). Prune out upright branches. Fire blight is a major problem; also susceptible to red spider mite, scale, and lace bug.
Herbicides: Dichlobenil, Simazine (both listed for genus).

Remarks. All species listed are good for erosion control on dry slopes (deep-rooted), for rocky ground, or for cascading over a wall. If grown in areas where fire blight is a problem, don't grow in large masses. Allow plenty of growing room so that stiff branch ends will not have to be pruned (important along walks, drives), as the stubby ends look bad. Deer-resistant. Some species, and probably all listed, tolerate environmental stress. Available in 1-gallon cans, 5-gallon cans (use if you can afford it), and probably balled-and-burlapped in some areas.

C. conspicua 'Decora'   12-15″ x 6-8′
Necklace Cotoneaster   **Zone 6**

Native to Western China. Evergreen, prostrate, moderate to fast growth. Small (¼″), oval, silvery-green leaves. Fairly good show of flowers followed by bright red, ⅜″ berries in profusion. Plant 3-4′ apart.

C. dammeri
Bearberry Cotoneaster
3-6" x 10'
Zone 6

Native to Central China. Evergreen, prostrate, fast growing, branches rooting as they grow (in moist soil). Will grow to 12" height with age. Leaves bright glossy green above, whitish beneath, 1", oval. Good show of flowers. Fruits bright red, ½", profuse. Plant 4-5' apart. C.d. 'Lowfast' (uncertain nomenclature, 12" x 10-15', vigorous, dark green leaves, gray-green beneath); C.d. 'Skogholmen' (6-12" x 3-5', moderately fast-growing, profuse flowers, fewer fruits).

C. horizontalis
Rock Cotoneaster
2-3' x 8-10'
Zone 5

Native to Western China. Semi-evergreen to deciduous, but out of leaf a short time. Spreading, mounding (with age), branches angled outwards. Moderate to fast-growing. Leaves dark green and glossy above, paler beneath, roundish, ½" long. Flowers pinkish-white, not very showy. Bright red shiny fruits make up for lack of leaves in winter. Tolerates environmental stress. Plant 4-5' apart. The most commonly sold of all groundcover Cotoneasters (though not necessarily the best). C.h. perpusilla (lower and more compact, ¼" leaves, more uniform growth, more fruit); C.h. 'Variegata' (leaves edged with white).

C. microphylla
Rockspray Cotoneaster
(Small-Leaved Cotoneaster)
2-3' x 6-10'
Zone 6

Native to the Himalayas. Evergreen, main branches trail and root, secondary branches more upright, dense, moderate to fast growth. Leaves ¼" long, dull dark green above, gray hairy beneath. Fruits rose red, larger than normal, profuse. Tolerates environmental stress. Plant 3-4' apart. C.m. 'Cochleata', (more prostrate and compact;) C.m. thymifolia (leaves ⅛-⅜").

Cyrtomium falcatum
Holly Fern
2' x 3'
Zone 9

Evergreen herbaceous perennial (fern) from eastern Asia. Polypody family (Polypodiaceae).

Characteristics. Symmetrical rosettes of fronds, angled upward and outward. Stiff fronds contain 2-4" long, glossy, dark green, leathery, holly-like leaflets; new growth is light green. The general appearance is very coarse for a fern.

Culture. Grows best in light soils, tolerates heavy clay, but must have good drainage; best in slightly acid soils,

tolerates slight alkalinity. Needs regular supply of water but don't overdo it on heavy clay soils. Partial to full shade; turns yellow and burns in full, hot sun. Belt 3 seashore (possibly Belt 2). Plant 12" to 18" apart. Susceptible to brown scale.

Remarks. Good for use in relatively small areas, narrow spaces, particularly in woodland settings. Easily available in pots or 1-gallon cans.

Varieties. C.f. 'Compactum' (shorter fronds, denser growth); C.f. 'Rochefordianum' (leaflets are even more holly-like).

Dichondra repens (D. carolinensis)
Dichondra (Ponyfoot)
½-3"
Zone 9

Evergreen herbaceous perennial native to the West Indies and to most of the southern United States from coast to coast. Morning-glory family (Convolvulaceae).

Characteristics. Thin, creeping runners grow above or slightly below the surface to form a ground-hugging, carpet-like mat; runners rooting at nodes (also increases by re-seeding). Fast-growing. Leaves are medium yellow-green to dark green, round, ¼" to 1" (depending on soil and light), somewhat resembling a horse's hoof.

Culture. Grows in various soils; most lush growth is in light, slightly acid soils with organic matter (not manure); tolerates heavy clay and slight alkalinity. Regular supply of moisture is necessary (shallow root system). Full sun to partial shade (taller and more lush in shade). Belt 3 seashore. Plant 2" square plugs 6" to 12" apart; can be planted from seed but requires much more attention to watering. Can be mown regularly; needs regular feeding (liquid fertilizer is best to avoid burning leaves with granules). Red spider mite, cutworms, slugs, snails, nematodes, and sugar beet fungus are potential problems.
Herbicides: Bensulide (use on either plugs or seed), Diphenamid (questionable on seed).

Remarks. Excellent between stepping stones or in other small areas, narrow spaces, good bulb cover and possible lawn substitute for small areas (used widely for lawns in California). Tolerates environmental stress, takes traffic well on light soils, less on heavier soils (do not step on leaves when stiff from frost). Available in flats and as seeds.

Duchesnea indica
Mock Strawberry (Indian Strawberry)
2-8"
Zone 6

Evergreen herbaceous perennial from southern Asia which has naturalized in many areas of the southern United States. Rose family (Rosaceae).

Characteristics. Clumps of growth send out runners that root and form a new plant at each node, creating a lush, dense mass of growth. Very fast growing and can be invasive. Leaves are medium to dark yellow-green (much the color of healthy St. Augustine grass), with three ovalish, coarsely toothed leaflets developing reddish tinges in winter and under dry conditions; appearance much like miniature strawberry plants. Yellow, ½-¾" strawberry-like flowers are scattered over the plants in spring through fall, not showy from a distance (pleasant up close), followed by tiny, bright red, strawberry-like fruits (edible but not tasty). Plants will have flowers and fruit at the same time.

Culture. Grows in any soil; best in loam with organic matter; tolerates poor soil. Will tolerate some dryness (lower and thinner); best with plenty of water. Full sun, partial shade (best in hot climates). Plant 12″ to 18″ apart. Requires frequent edge trimming. Rust can be a problem (Benomyl has given good control—don't use where children might eat fruits), but usually grows out of it in a month or so.
Herbicides: EPTC

Remarks. Useful in small or large areas, narrow spaces, between stepping stones, and as a bulb cover. Deer-resistant. Available in flats or pots, although not easily found in some areas. Sometimes confused with Fragaria chiloensis and Potentilla crantzii.

Euonymus fortunei (E. radicans)   18-24″ x 3-4′
Wintercreeper   **Zone 6**

Evergreen woody sub-shrub or vine from China. Bittersweet family (Celastraceae).

Characteristics. Mounding, with trailing branches that root when they touch the ground; will climb walls and into shrubs and trees (adheres by aerial rootlets). Slow-growing at first, then fast. Leaves dark, glossy green, 1-2″ long, variable in size and shape, edged with rounded teeth.

Culture. Grows in most well-drained soils, best with organic matter, tolerates poor soil. Prefers a regular supply of water. Sun to full shade, tolerates heat. Belt 1 seashore. Plant 24″ apart. Euonymus scale is a severe problem in hot, dry areas.
Herbicides: DCPA (listed for genus), Dichlobenil (listed for genus), EPTC (listed for genus), Trifluralin.

Remarks. Useful on rocky slopes (larger, faster-growing varieties), large or small areas (depending on variety), narrow spaces (small varieties), for cascading over a wall. Do not use if scale is a severe problem in your area. Tolerates environmental stress. All parts of the plant are poisonous if eaten. Available in flats (some varieties) or 1-gallon cans.

Varieties

E.f. 'Azusa': Prostrate, small dark green leaves turn maroon in winter.

E.f. 'Coloratus' (Purple Wintercreeper): One of the most commonly available. Vigorous, rambling vine, 12-24″ x 3-4′. Leaves 1″ long, bright green turning dark purplish in fall and winter.

E.f. 'Emerald Cushion': Mounding, small-leaved.

E.f. 'Gracilis' (E.f. variegata, E.f. 'Argenteo-marginatus', E.f. 'Silver Edge', E.f. 'Argenteo-variegata', E. radicans argenteo-variegata): Not as vigorous as the species. Leaves have white or creamy variegation on edges, turning pinkish in winter.

E.f. 'Kewensis' (Kew Wintercreeper): Low creeping habit, 2″ high, the smallest of all; slow-growing; leaves ¼″ long. Plant 12″ to 18″ apart. Use in small areas only, between stepping stones.

E.f. 'Longwood': Low, spreading vine, 6-8″ high, wiry branches form a dense mat. Tiny, oval, dark green leaves. Plant 18″ to 24″ apart. Good for small areas.

E.f. 'Minimus' (Baby Wintercreeper): Similar to E.f. 'Kewensis', 2″ high, creeping, ½″ long leaves. Also in a white variegated form.

E.f. radicans (Common Wintercreeper): Trailing, 4″ high. Leaves ½-1″ long, dark green.

E.f. vegetus (Bigleaf Wintercreeper): Tallest growing, 3-4′, but can be kept lower, vigorous. Leaves larger, rounder, more leathery, coarser teeth. Decorative fruits with orange seeds.

Festuca ovina 'Glauca'
   (F. glauca)   **6-10″ x 10-12″**
Blue Fescue (Dwarf Blue Fescue)   **Zone 5**

Evergreen perennial grass of the grass family (Gramineae).

Characteristics. Grows in fountain-like tufts or clumps. Thin, wire-like leaves are light silvery blue.

Culture. Must have light, very well-drained soil; tolerates poor and rocky soils, dies out in center of clump in heavy clay. Best in dry conditions; will not tolerate wet soils. Full sun to very light shade. Belt 2 seashore. Plant 6″ to 12″ apart (close spacing needed for solid cover, wider spacing for "dot" effect). Trim off old flower heads for best appearance, shear off foliage to rejuvenate.

Remarks. Best used in small areas, narrow spaces, good for creating geometric patterns of dots. Interesting in combination with Cerastium tomentosum or when contrasted with dark green plants. For non-traffic areas. Available in flats, pots, 1-gallon cans.

Fragaria (fruiting varieties)   **6-12″**
Strawberry   **Zone 2 (variable depending on variety)**

Evergreen herbaceous perennials. The fruiting forms grown today are hybrids between F. chiloensis and F. virginiana. Rose family (Rosaceae).

Characteristics. Rosettes of foliage produce surface runners that root and form new plants at each node; runners interlace to form a mass of growth. Types without runners are not as suitable for groundcover use. Very fast-growing. Leaves have three dark green leaflets, varying from 1½″ to about 4″ long depending on variety, developing reddish tints in winter. Flowers are white, ½-¾″ across, in clusters, usually not showy, at different times of year depending on variety, followed by strawberries (what else).

Culture. Best grown in light, well-drained, fertile, slightly acid soils with plenty of organic matter; will tolerate heavy clay with reasonable drainage, tolerates slight alkalinity (iron chlorosis is a problem if too alkaline). Needs regular watering (can be overwatered on clay soils), particularly in hot summers. Full sun to partial shade (best flowering and fruiting is in sun). Plant 12″ to 18″ apart, do not set crown too low or it may rot. Fertilize regularly, can be mown or sheared high in early spring to rejuvenate (fertilize afterwards). Grubs, red stele fungus, and verticillium wilt all can be a problem.
Herbicides: DCPA (slight stunting of some varieties, quickly outgrown), Diphenamid (some varieties stunted, quickly outgrown, best applied when in active growth, wait 60 days before eating fruit), EPTC.

Remarks. Good for small or fairly large areas, narrow spaces, bulb cover. Available in flats, pots, bare-root (plant in spring or fall). Among the many fruiting varieties, 'Florida Ninety', 'Earlibelle', and 'Headline' all are good in the South.

F. chiloensis	6-8″

Sand Strawberry (Wild Strawberry, Ornamental Strawberry)   **Zones 7-8**

Native to the west coast of North and South America. Leaflets smaller than fruiting varieties, glossy. Fruit is small and sparsely produced. Best in light, slightly acid soils. Will tolerate some dryness; best with regular watering. Full sun in cool climates (with plenty of water), partial shade in hot climates. Belt 1 seashore.

Herbicides: Bensulide, DCPA (see comments above), EPTC. *Not recommended:* Diphenamid.

Tolerates environmental stress and a little traffic. F. 'Number 25' is a hybrid between F. chiloensis and a fruiting variety, grows taller (to 12″ or 15″), all parts are larger than F. chiloensis, fruit is better; does not tolerate traffic.

Gardenia jasminoides 'Radicans'
(G. radicans)   **18-24″ x 2-3′**
Dwarf Gardenia (Dwarf Cape Jasmine)   **Zones 8-9**

Evergreen woody shrub native to China. Coffee family (Rubiaceae).

Characteristics. Spreading, mounding growth. Slow to moderate growth rate. Leaves dark, glossy green, 1-1½″ long by ½-¾″ wide, pointed, frequently irregularly streaked with white variegation on some leaves. Flowers are white, fading to brownish on old flowers, 1-1½″ across, double, showy, late spring to early summer, very fragrant.

Culture. Best grown in light, well-drained, acid soils with plenty of organic matter, tolerates slight alkalinity and heavy clay (with drainage), shows iron chlorosis if too alkaline. Needs plenty of water. Full sun, partial shade in hot climates and on sandy soils. Plant 18″ to 24″ apart. Best with regular feeding (acid fertilizer). Has problems with white fly, scale, nematodes.

Herbicides: Dichlobenil (listed for genus), EPTC.

Remarks. Useful in small areas, narrow spaces, near entrances or other areas where people can enjoy the fragrance. Available in 1-gallon cans.

Gelsemium sempervirens   2-3′
Carolina Jessamine (Carolina Jasmine)   **Zone 7**

Evergreen woody vine native to the southern United States and Central America. Logania family (Loganiaceae).

Characteristics. A twining vine that forms mounds of growth when used as a groundcover. Fast-growing (sometimes a little slow starting). Leaves are light to medium yellow-green, shiny, 2-3″ long, narrowly lance-shaped, developing slight reddish tints in winter. Bright yellow, 1″ long, clustered, trumpet-shaped flowers in profusion in late winter to early spring (occasional flowers in the fall), lightly fragrant.

Culture. Grows in most soils, best in acid soils with organic matter. Needs regular watering. Full sun to partial shade. Plant 2′ to 4′ apart. Trim occasionally for bushiness. Essentially pest-free.

Herbicides: EPTC.

Remarks. Useful in small or large areas, for cascading over a wall. Will climb into shrubs and trees but not up a wall. Very deer-resistant. All parts are poisonous when eaten, and can also cause dermatitis in people prone to the disease. Very widely grown as a vine; little used as a groundcover (although eminently suitable); commonly available in 1-gallon cans.

Varieties. G.s. 'Flore-pleno' (double-flowered).

Hedera helix   12-15″
English Ivy   **Zone 6**

Probably the most commonly grown groundcover in the South. Evergreen woody vine from Europe. Aralia or Ginseng family (Araliaceae).

Characteristics. Trailing, rooting stems form a dense, lush mass of leaves, eventually developing a thick mat of intertwined stems. Slow to start (for a year or so), then moderately fast-growing. Leaves dark, dull green, 2-4″ wide and long, 3- to 5- lobed like a simplified maple leaf; new growth is bright green.

Culture. Adaptable to most soils, best with good drainage and plenty of organic matter; tolerates poor soils. Prefers plenty of water, tolerates dryness (except in full sun). Partial to full shade; tolerates full sun with water in cool climates (leaves burn in sun in hot climates); tolerates tree root competition. Belt 2 seashore. Plant 12″ to 18″ apart. Requires regular edge trimming; can be sheared heavily to rejuvenate in spring. Susceptible to scale, aphids.

Herbicides: Bensulide (listed for genus), Dichlobenil (partial injury with recovery), Diphenamid, DCPA, EPTC, Simazine (injury on sandy soils, safer on clay), Trifluralin.

Remarks. Good for small or large areas, narrow spaces, shady slopes (deep-rooted), cascading over a wall. Smaller-leaved varieties are better for narrow spaces, between stepping stones. Will climb walls, trees, and shrubs, but can be easily controlled. Strongly deer-resistant and tolerant of environmental stress. Leaves and berries are poisonous if eaten and can cause dermatitis in sensitive people. Commonly available in flats, pots, 1-gallon cans, and easily grown by cuttings from neighbors.

The varieties available, both green and variegated, are too numerous to mention. Most have much smaller leaves, variously shaped, are slower-growing, and are best suited to small areas, even between stepping stones. One commonly available variety is H.h. 'Hahns Self-Branching' (H.h. hahnii), with slightly smaller, lighter green leaves forming a denser mat.

H. canariensis	12-15″
Algerian Ivy	**Zones 8-9**

Leaves 5-8″ across, shiny, mostly 3-lobed, stems and leaf stalks burgundy red. Tolerates more sun but needs plenty of moisture; tolerates poor drainage. Belt 1 seashore. Tolerates environmental stress. Also has a variegated form (H.c. 'Variegata').
Herbicides: same as for H. helix.

Heuchera sanguinea	12″ x 12″
Coral Bells	**Zone 4**

Evergreen herbaceous perennial native to Arizona, New Mexico, and Mexico. Saxifrage family (Saxifragaceae).

Characteristics. Non-spreading, dense clumps of foliage. Dark olive-green, rounded, 1-2″ leaves have scalloped edges, shaped much like geranium leaves. Drooping flowers are bell-shaped, ½″ long, bright red or coral pink, in open-branched spikes on thin, erect stems to 24″, very showy, spring and summer, long-blooming.

Culture. Grows best in light, well-drained alkaline soils with organic matter; does poorly in heavy clay. Requires plenty of water (shallow-rooted). Full sun (cooler climates) to partial shade (hot climates). Belt 2 seashore. Plant 6″ to 12″ apart. Trim off old flower spikes for neatness. Susceptible to fungus diseases in wet soils.
Herbicides: Bensulide (listed for genus).

Remarks. Use in small areas and narrow spaces only. Available in pots.

Varieties. Many horticultural varieties are available with flowers ranging from white to varying shades of red and pink.

Hypericum calycinum	12-18″
Dwarf Hypericum (Creeping	
St. Johns-wort, Aaronsbeard	
St. Johns-wort)	**Zones 6-7**

Evergreen to semi-evergreen (cold climates) semi-woody shrub from southeastern Europe and Asia Minor. St. Johns-wort family (Hypericaceae).

Characteristics. Spreading branches rooting when they touch the ground and underground runners combine to form mounds of dense growth. Moderate to fast-growing; can be invasive. Leaves are medium yellow-green, 2-4″ long, oblong, with purplish tinges in winter. Bright yellow, 3″ flowers in summer, showy, long-blooming.

Culture. Grows in any soil, tolerates poor soil. Best with plenty of moisture, tolerates some dryness and wetness. Full sun to partial shade (hot climates). Not at its best in hottest areas, even in shade. Plant 12″ to 18″ apart. Needs trimming for bushiness, shear tops if growth becomes too rank, do not use green manures.
Herbicides: Bensulide (listed for genus), DCPA (listed for genus), Diphenamid, Simazine (partial injury), Trifluralin.

Remarks. Useful in large areas or small areas (if confined), narrow spaces, good on slopes if properly watered. Tolerates environmental stress. Available in flats and 1-gallon cans.

Iberis sempervirens	8-12″ x 1½-2′
Evergreen Candytuft	**Zone 4**

Evergreen herbaceous to semi-woody perennial from Crete. Mustard family (Cruciferae).

Characteristics. Low, spreading stems root as they touch the ground forming lush, dense mounds of growth. Fast-growing. Narrow, dark green leaves are 1½″ long. Small pure white flowers grow in flat clusters, heavily produced in spring through early summer and sporadically in winter in mild areas; very showy.

Culture. Grows in any well-drained soil with a regular supply of water. Full sun to partial shade. Belt 2 seashore. Plant 12″ to 18″ apart. Trim for bushiness and to remove old flowers.
Herbicides: Bensulide (listed for genus).

Remarks. Useful in small areas, narrow spaces, for cascading over a wall. Tolerates environmental stress. Available in flats or pots and easily grown from seed.

Varieties. Many are available: I.s. 'Little Cushion' (3-6″ x 12″); I.s. 'Little Gem' (4-6″); I.s. 'Snowflake' (4-12″ x 2-3′, larger flower clusters, bloom scattered throughout year in mild climates, one of the best varieties).

Ilex
Holly

Evergreen woody shrubs of the Holly family (Aquifoliaceae).

Characteristics. See individual species listing.

Culture. Best growth is in rich, well-drained, acid soil with plenty of organic matter; tolerate slight alkalinity. Need plenty of water. Full sun to partial shade. Plant 18″ apart. The species listed here can be sheared. Susceptible to various types of scale.

Herbicides: Bensulide (listed for genus), EPTC (listed for I. crenata), Trifluralin (listed for I. crenata). *Do not use* on any of listed species: Dichlobenil.

Remarks. Leaves and berries of all species are poisonous if eaten. All those listed are available in 1-gallon cans and sometimes balled-and-burlapped.

I. cornuta 'Rotunda'	18″ x 24″
Dwarf Chinese Holly	**Zone 7**

Dense, compact mound of foliage. Slow-growing. Leaves are dark olive-green with several sharp spine-like teeth, 2-3″ long. Does not produce fruit. Can become heavily infested with tea scale on underside of leaf (difficult to eliminate because of location). Difficult to weed because of spiny leaves. Best used in small areas (particularly if scale is a problem in your location), keep away from walkways (spiny leaves), good traffic control barrier.

I. crenata 'Helleri'	12-18″ x 24″
Dwarf Japanese Holly	**Zone 6**

Dense, compact mound of ½″ long, dark green leaves. Slow-growing. Looks more like a boxwood than a holly. Berries not significant. Belt 2 seashore. Useful in large or small areas, narrow spaces. Tolerates environmental stress. Can reach 4′ with age but easily kept lower.

I. vomitoria 'Nana'	18″ x 2-2½′
Dwarf Yaupon	**Zone 7**

Dense, compact mound of narrow, oval, ½-¾″ long, dark olive-green leaves with rounded teeth. Slow-growing. Tolerates more alkalinity than other species, tolerates some wetness. Useful in large or small areas and narrow spaces. *I.v. 'Stokes'* is smaller, about 12″ high.

Juniperus
Juniper

Evergreen woody shrubs of the Pine family (Pinaceae).

Characteristics. See individual species listings.

Culture. Grow in most soils as long as they are well-drained, best in light soils, tolerate poor soil. Drought-tolerant; will accept regular watering with drainage. Full sun to very light shade. Weed control is important because of wide spacings; use fertilizer sparingly. Susceptible to cedar apple rust (*do not plant* near Apple,

Cotoneaster, Hawthorn), spider mites, twig borers, Juniper blight.

Herbicides: these are all listed for the genus— Bensulide, DCPA, Dichlobenil, Diphenamid, EPTC, Simazine, Trifluralin.

Remarks. Useful in large and small areas, for cascading over a wall, on hot, dry slopes. If planted too close to paved areas, branch ends must be trimmed, which somewhat destroys the beauty of the natural form. Too close a spacing causes crowded plants to die out (removal of every other one solves the problem). Available in 1-gallon cans and sometimes balled-and-burlapped. Deer-resistant and tolerant of environmental stress.

J. chinensis sargentii (J. sargentii)	12″ x 8-10′
Sargent Juniper	**Zone 5**

Native to northern coastal Japan. Wide-spreading, forming a dense, mounded mat. Slow-growing. Leaves tiny, scale-like, sharp pointed, gray-green. Belt 2 seashore. Plant 3′ to 4′ apart.

Herbicides: see listing above; Trifluralin (listed for J. chinensis). Good for dry slopes. J.c.s. 'Glauca' has blue-green foliage.

J. conferta (J. litoralis)	12-24″ x 6-8′
Shore Juniper	**Zone 6**

Native to coastal Japan. Widely trailing to form an uneven, low-growing mat with branchlets pointing upward. Leaves needle-like but soft, bright green to gray-green. Slow-growing. Not at its best in the hottest areas of zones 9 and 10. Prefers sandy, very well-drained, even poor soils. Belt 1 seashore. Plant 2′ to 3′ apart.

Herbicides: See listing under genus; Trifluralin (listed for this species). J.c. 'Blue Pacific' has more blue-green foliage, tolerates a little more heat.

J. horizontalis (J. prostrata)	12-18″ x 8′
Prostrate Juniper (Creeping Juniper)	**Zone 2**

Native to the northeastern United States. Habit of growth varies from plants with long, prostrate rooting branches to those that are more compact (the varieties are less variable). Moderate rate of growth. Leaves are scale-like, bluish-green (some forms turn purplish in winter), sharp-pointed. Belt 2 seashore. Plant 3′ to 4′ apart. Good for dry slopes.

J.h. 'Bar Harbor' (Bar Harbor Juniper, 6-12″ x 10′, very flat-growing, moderate to fast growth rate, blue-gray leaves turn purplish in winter); J.h. 'Douglasii' (Waukegan Juniper, 12-18″ x 10′ or more, trailing, moderate to fast-growing, steel blue leaves turn purplish in winter, plant 4′ to 5′ apart); J.h. 'Plumosa' (Andorra

Juniper, 12-18" x 8', uniformly spreading branches with upright branchlets, compact, gray-green, turning purple in winter, plant 3' to 4' apart); J.h. 'Wiltonii' (Blue Rug Juniper, 4-6" x 8-10', flattest growing of all, leaves are silvery-blue-green with slight purplish tints in winter, plant 4' to 5' apart); J.h. 'Emerald' (12" x 8', low, mat-like growth, rich, bright green leaves).

J. procumbens (J. chinensis   **2-3' x 10-20'**
  procumbens)
Japanese Garden Juniper   **Zone 6**

Native to Japan. Spreading, prostrate, dense, mounding in the center. Slow-growing. Leaves are scale-like, sharp-pointed, bluish-green. Belt 2 seashore. Plant 4' to 5' apart. J.p. 'Nana' 12" x 4-5', very dense, prostrate, slightly mounding in center, bluish-gray, plant 2' apart, can be used in smaller areas than most other species and varieties.

J. sabina 'Tamariscifolia'   **18-24" x 10'-15'**
  (J. tamariscifolia)
Tam Juniper (Tamarix Juniper)   **Zone 5**

Native to Europe and Siberia. Symmetrically spreading branches, mounded, dense. Slow to moderate growth rate. Leaves scale-like, sharp-pointed, medium green to slightly bluish-green. Belt 2 seashore. Plant 4' to 5' apart. J.s. 'Broadmoor' (12-14" x 10', prostrate and mounding, dense, bright green leaves); J.s. 'Buffalo' (12" x 8', prostrate, bright green leaves).

J. virginiana 'Silver Spreader'   **18-24" x 6-8'**
  (J. virginiana 'Prostrata')
                                           Zone 5

Spreading habit with feathery foliage. Leaves scale-like, silvery-green turning dark green on older branches. Plant 3' to 4' apart.
  Herbicides: See list under genus; Trifluralin (listed for this variety).

Liriope muscari   **12-15" x 18-24"**
Liriope (Big Blue Lily-turf)   **Zones 6-7**

Evergreen herbaceous perennial from Japan and China. Lily family (Liliaceae).

Characteristics. Grass-like clumps or tufts of arching leaves (does not spread by runners). Slow-growing. Leaves are very dark green (new growth bright green), glossy, ½" wide by 18" long (varying in length). Small, lilac-purple flowers in dense, erect spikes mostly among the leaves on older plants in summer; semi-showy (varieties flower more profusely).

Culture. Grows in most well-drained soils. Best with plenty of water, tolerates some wetness (not soggy) and some dryness. Full sun (cool climates, with water), partial to full shade (hot climates). Belt 3 seashore. Plant 8" to 12" apart. Old unsightly leaves made ragged by winter can be sheared off near the ground in spring before new growth. Does not require much fertilizer (except where root competition is strong). Weed control is sometimes a continuing problem in the sun. Snails and slugs occasionally cause damage.
  Herbicides: EPTC.

Remarks. There is much confusion in the nursery trade in the offering of Liriope. Apparently, several different varieties are sold as L. muscari. All are usually labeled simply, Liriope. This presents no real problem, as they all require the same culture and are similar in characteristics. Liriope is too often used as a border only; it is best used in small to moderately large areas and narrow spaces. Leaf tips will turn brown in soggy and excessively salty soils and in severe cold. Tolerates environmental stress. Available in pots, 1-gallon cans and from neighbors by division of clumps. Common throughout the South.

Varieties. Many exist; here are some common ones: L.m. 'Big Blue' (commonly used name for the species); L.m. 'Christmas Tree' (L.m. 'Monroe #2', light violet flowers on spikes well above foliage, very showy); L.m. 'Lilac Beauty' (¾" wide leaves, lilac-colored flowers); L.m. 'Majestic' (10-12" high, leaves up to ½" wide by 13" long, less vigorous, violet flowers, probably one of the varieties often sold as 'Big Blue'); L.m. 'Monroe White' (L.m. 'Monroe #1', leaves burn in the sun, white flowers); L.m. 'Variegata' (yellow or whitish-yellow leaf margins when young, green with age, dark violet flowers).

L. spicata   **6-12"**
Creeping Lily-turf   **Zone 5**

Grass-like clumps spreading by underground stems. Moderate growth rate. Leaves are ¼" wide, dark green, not as erect as L. muscari. Flowers pale lilac to whitish, held just above the foliage. Tolerates more drought and sun than L. muscari. Belt 2 seashore. Not as readily available.

For more on Liriope, see "The Lilyturfs in Gardens" by H. Harold Hume and B.Y. Morrison, *The American Horticultural Magazine*, Vol. 46, #3, July 1967, pp. 188-198.

Lonicera japonica 'Halliana'   **18-24"**
Hall's Honeysuckle (Hall's
  Japanese Honeysuckle)   **Zone 5**

Evergreen woody vine from Asia. Honeysuckle family (Caprifoliaceae).

Characteristics. Vigorous twining vine forming irregular mounds of growth, climbing if given support, branches root when they touch the ground. Very fast-growing. Leaves are oval to oblong, 3″ long, dark green. Flowers are white, fading to pale yellow, showy, very sweetly fragrant, late spring to summer.

Culture. Grows in almost any soil, tolerates poor drainage. Somewhat drought-tolerant, but best with plenty of water; tolerates wet conditions. Full sun to partial shade. Belt 2 seashore. Plant 18″ to 24″ apart. Trim occasionally for bushiness, shear and remove undergrowth annually if in a fire-prone area.
Herbicides: DCPA (listed for genus), Dichlobenil (listed for genus), EPTC, Trifluralin (listed for genus).

Remarks. Will climb into shrubs and trees. Best used in large areas, on steep slopes, cascading over a wall, in areas where people can enjoy the fragrance. Tolerates environmental stress. Has escaped and become a weed in many areas of the South. Available in flats, pots, 1-gallon cans. Common throughout the South.

Varieties. L.j. chinensis (Purple Japanese Honeysuckle), young leaves and outside of flowers reddish-purple, mature leaves purplish underneath.

Lysimachia nummularia   2-4″
Moneywort (Creeping Charlie, Creeping Jenny)   **Zone 4**

Evergreen herbaceous perennial native to Europe. Primrose family (Primulaceae).

Characteristics. Long creeping stems hug the ground, rooting as they grow, forming a flat mat. Very fast-growing. Round, ½-¾″ leaves are light to medium yellow-green, in pairs along the stem. Flowers are yellow, ¾″ across, star-shaped, in summer, scattered and produced irregularly, if at all.

Culture. Grows well in heavy soils or loam; tolerates poorly drained, soggy soils (even grows underwater in an aquarium). Must have abundant water supply. Best in partial to full shade, tolerates some sun in heavy moist soils. Plant 12″ to 18″ apart. Requires frequent edge trimming; weeds can be a problem in sunny locations. Susceptible to red spider mite.

Remarks. Best used in small areas and narrow spaces only, between stepping stones, as a bulb cover, cascading over a wall. Deer-resistant. A weedy lawn pest in the North. Can be walked on, but not regularly. Available in flats and pots.

Malephora
Iceplant

Evergreen succulent perennials from South Africa. Iceplant or Carpetweed family (Aizoaceae). Much name confusion exists among the iceplants (often grouped under the name Mesembryanthemum).

Characteristics. See individual species listing.

Culture. Need light well-drained soil; tolerate poor or rocky soil. Drought-tolerant but can be watered regularly with sharp drainage. Full sun. Many of the iceplants can tolerate Belt 1 seashore conditions. Plant 12″ to 18″ apart. May be cut back every few years to renew growth.
Herbicides: These are all listed for iceplants in general—Bensulide, Diphenamid (possible slight injury), EPTC.

Remarks. Useful in small areas, narrow spaces. Tolerate environmental stress. Available in flats or pots. Easily propagated from cuttings.

M. crocea (Hymenocyclus croceus)   6-12″
Croceum Iceplant   **Zone 8**

Mounded growth sends out trailing, rooting stems. Fast-growing. Leaves are 1-2″ long, rod-like, triangular in cross-section, smooth, gray-green, succulent. Flowers are coppery-yellow, 1″ across, Aster-like, sparsely produced much of the year, heaviest in spring. Can be used on hot, dry slopes. M.c. purpureo-crocea has coppery-red flowers, bluish-green leaves.

M. luteola (Hymenocyclus luteolus)   6-12″
Yellow Trailing Iceplant   **Zone 9**

Mounded growth sending out short, trailing stems. Fast-growing. Leaves are 1½″ long, rod-like, triangular in cross-section, smooth, light green to gray-green. Flowers are yellow, 1″ across, Aster-like, heaviest in summer and scattered during much of the year.
Herbicides: In addition to those listed above—Trifluralin. *Not recommended:* DCPA, Dichlobenil, Simazine.

Nepeta hederacea (Glecoma hederacea)   3-6″
Ground Ivy (Gill-over-the-Ground)   **Zone 4**

Evergreen herbaceous perennial from Europe and Asia. Mint family (Labiatae).

Characteristics. Creeping, rooting stems form a dense mat of growth. Very fast-growing, can be invasive. Leaves are bright medium green, rounded, 1-1½″, with coarsely scalloped edges. Flowers are light blue, 1″ across, in few-flowered clusters among the leaves in spring and summer.

Culture. Grows in most soils, best in loam. Needs plenty of water. Best in partial to full shade; tolerates some sun with regular watering. Belt 3 seashore. Plant 12″ to 18″ apart. Requires frequent edge trimming.

Remarks. Good in small areas, narrow spaces, between stepping stones, as a bulb cover. Tolerates environmental stress. Leaves are poisonous if eaten in large quantities. Available in flats, pots.

Varieties. N.h. variegata has gray-green leaves with creamy-white edges.

Ophiopogon japonicus (Mondo japonicum)   6-12″ x 8-12″
Monkey Grass (Mondo Grass, Dwarf Lily-turf)   **Zones 7-8**

Evergreen herbaceous perennial from Japan and Korea. Lily family (Liliaceae).

Characteristics. Grass-like clumps spread by underground runners to form a dense billowy mass of fine foliage. Slow to start, then moderate growth rate after a year or two. Grass-like leaves are ⅛″ wide, very dark-green. Tiny violet or blue-violet flowers are sometimes sparsely produced on short spikes among the foliage in early summer; not showy.

Culture. Grows in any soil but best in rich loam; tolerates poor drainage. Somewhat drought-tolerant; best with plenty of water. Full sun to partial shade (hot climates), more lush in shade. Belt 2 seashore. Plant 6″ to 12″ apart, best at close spacing. Bermuda grass can be a weed problem in sunny areas.
Herbicides: EPTC.

Remarks. Good for small or large areas, narrow spaces, bulb cover. Large mature masses are extremely attractive, particularly when the wind ripples across the surface. Looks good when contrasted with light-foliaged plants such as Liriope muscari 'Variegata'. Tolerates environmental stress and a little traffic (although not easy to walk through). A very tough plant, and worthy of other uses besides the typical border. Available in flats, pots, 1-gallon cans, or from neighbors by division of clumps. A very common plant thoughout the South.

Pachysandra terminalis   6-12″
Pachysandra (Japanese Spurge)   **Zone 6**

Evergreen herbaceous perennial or sub-shrub from Japan. Boxwood family (Buxaceae).

Characteristics. Spreads by underground runners sending up erect stems with clusters of leaves at the tips, forming a dense mass of growth, uniform in height. Moderate rate of growth. Spoon-shaped, ovalish 1-3″ long leaves are medium to dark green, shiny, coarsely toothed on upper end. Small white flowers on short, upright spikes slightly above the foliage are produced in summer, if at all (some plantings do not flower), followed by white berries (not showy).

Culture. Needs rich, slightly acid soil with plenty of organic matter. Requires plenty of water, particularly when young. Partial to full shade (leaves turn yellow in full sun). Belt 2 seashore; will not tolerate wind. Plant 6″ to 12″ apart. Pinch or trim lightly in spring for bushiness, best with regular feeding. Susceptible to Euonymus scale (particularly in sunny dry areas), root rot.
Herbicides: Bensulide (listed for genus), DCPA, Diphenamid, EPTC, Trifluralin.

Remarks. Useful in large or small areas, narrow spaces, as a bulb cover (vigorous bulbs), on steep slopes.

Competes well with tree roots. Tolerates environmental stress. Available in flats, pots, 1-gallon cans.

Varieties. P.t. 'Variegata' has lighter green leaves with white edge variegation.

Paxistima canbyi (Pachistima canbyi)   9-12″
Canby Paxistima (Rat-Stripper)   **Zone 6**

Most commonly found listed as *Pachistima*, although a recent name change invalidates this spelling. Evergreen shrub native to the eastern United States. Bittersweet family (Celastraceae).

Characteristics. Low, compact, dense, mounding form with trailing, rooting branches. Slow-growing. Leaves are dark green, turning bronzy in fall, shiny, leathery, ½-1″ long, ¼″ wide, on wiry stems.

Culture. Needs a well-drained, acid (pH 4.5-5.5), rich soil with plenty of organic matter; tolerates rocky soil. Requires plenty of water. Full sun (cool areas); partial shade (warm areas). Plant 12″ apart. Can be trimmed regularly.
Herbicides: Dichlobenil (listed for genus).

Remarks. Best for small areas, narrow spaces. Available in pots, 1-gallon cans.

Phlox subulata   6″ x 2′
Moss-Pink (Ground-Pink)   **Zone 3**

Evergreen semi-woody perennial native to the eastern United States. Phlox family (Polemoniaceae).

Characteristics. Prostrate, creeping, rooting stems form a mat of growth. Fast-growing. Leaves are needle-like, ½″ long, stiff, bright olive-green. Flowers are bright pink or white, star-like, ¾″ across, in profuse masses in spring.

Culture. Best in light, well-drained soils; tolerates poor, rocky soil and heavy clay (with drainage). Tolerates some dryness (except on lightest soils); best with regular watering. Full sun. Plant 12″ to 18″ apart. Trim back about one-half after flowering to provide fresh growth.
Herbicides: Trifluralin (listed for genus).

Remarks. Best in small areas, narrow spaces, as a bulb cover, for cascading over a wall. Tolerates environmental stress. Old plants may die out in the center (remove and replant). Available in pots and 1-gallon cans.

Varieties. Many horticultural varieties are available and are more commonly sold than the species: P.s. 'Alexanders Surprise' (pink flowers, often blooms again in fall); P.s. 'Emerald Cushion' (lower growing, pink flowers); P.s. 'Brilliant' (dark pink to nearly red flowers); P.s. 'Blue Hills' (blue flowers); P.s. 'Sky Blue' (blue flowers); P.s. alba (white flowers).

Pittosporum tobira 'Wheelers Dwarf'   **3' x 4'**
(P.t. 'Wheeleri')
Wheeler's Dwarf Pittosporum   **Zones 8-9**

Evergreen woody shrub of the Pittosporum family (Pittosporaceae). Because this is a very new introduction, some of the information presented here has not been totally tested but appears to be reasonably sound.

Characteristics. Dense, compact, neat mound. Slow-growing. Leaves are leathery, shiny, 1½-2½" long by ½-¾" wide, medium to dark green, new growth is light green. Flowers are creamy-white, ½" across in clusters at branch tips, early spring, not showy from a distance but pleasant up close because of orange blossom-like fragrance.

Culture. Grows in most well-drained soils; best in heavy soils, alkaline to slightly acid. Tolerates some dryness but best with regular watering. Full sun to partial shade; tolerates heat. Belt 1 seashore (P. tobira). Plant 2' apart. Can be clipped to keep low (not necessary for compactness), weeds can be a problem because of slow growth. Susceptible to aphids, scale.

Remarks. Useful in small areas (clipped) or large areas. Tolerates environmental stress. Available in 1-gallon cans (plants are very small).

Polygonum capitatum   **6-8"**
Pinkhead Knotweed (Pink
Fleece-Flower)   **Zones 9-10**

Evergreen (tender) perennial from the Himalayas. Rhubarb or Buckwheat family (Polygonaceae).

Characteristics. Trailing, rooting branches form a low mat of growth. Fast-growing. Leaves are oval, pointed, 1½" long, dark bronzy-green with a blackish-green V-shaped pattern. Tiny flowers are bright pink in dense, round, button-like, ½-¾" heads, profuse most of the year.

Culture. Grows well in heavy, slightly alkaline soils; tolerates poor soil. Needs plenty of water. Full sun to light shade. Plant 12" apart.

Remarks. Freezes below about 28° but reseeds itself and returns in spring. Useful in small areas, narrow spaces. No traffic; tolerates environmental stress. Available in flats.

Potentilla crantzii (P. verna)   **4-8"**
Spring Cinquefoil   **Zone 6**

Evergreen herbaceous perennial from Europe. Rose family (Rosaceae). Most commonly sold under the name P. verna, a name now invalidated by a recent change.

Characteristics. Creeping, rooting runners grow flat on the ground in all directions from tufts of foliage forming a dense, even mass of growth. Fast-growing. Leaves have five leaflets, palmately arranged, medium yellow-green, wedge-shaped, ½-¾" long, coarsely toothed. Flowers are bright yellow, ½" across, scattered over the foliage in spring through fall, no large quantity at any one time.

Culture. Grows in most well-drained soils. Best with plenty of water. Full sun if regularly watered; best in partial shade (particularly in hot climates). Plant 12" to 18" apart. Requires regular edge trimming, can be mown high in spring to promote lush new growth.
Herbicides: Diphenamid (partial stunting and chlorosis with quick recovery), EPTC, Trifluralin (listed for genus).

Remarks. Good for small or large areas, narrow spaces, as a bulb cover, between stepping stones. Best when separated from St. Augustine grass by paving because the two are much the same color. Easily confused with Duchesnea indica at a glance (Duchesnea has three leaflets, red fruits). The two can be mixed if the necessary quantity of one or the other is not available. Tolerates environmental stress. Available in flats and pots.

P. cinerea   **2-4"**
Rusty Cinquefoil (Alpine Cinquefoil)   **Zone 4**

Native to the Alps. Leaves oblong, gray, hairy, toothed. Pale yellow flowers. Best grown in cooler parts of the South.

P. tridentata   **2-12"**
Wineleaf Cinquefoil   **Zone 3**

Native from Greenland to Georgia. Semi-woody, three dark green leaflets, ½-1" long. Flowers are white, ¼" across. In the cooler parts of the South it can be grown in full sun. Tolerates dry, rocky soil, prefers acid soil.

Pyracantha koidzumi 'Santa Cruz'   **3'**
(P. 'Santa Cruz Prostrata')
Santa Cruz Pyracantha   **Zone 8**

Evergreen woody shrub in the Rose family (Rosaceae).

Characteristics. Stiff, thorny, spreading to occasionally erect branches. Moderate growth rate. Leaves are dark green, shiny, 1½"-2" long, oval, pointed, toothed. Flowers are white, ¼" across in many-flowered clusters in spring, fairly showy, followed by bright red, ¼" berries, showy in late fall and winter, relished by birds.

Culture. Grows best in well-drained, heavy, neutral to slightly alkaline soils. Tolerates some dryness but prefers regular watering. Full sun. Possibly Belt 3 seashore. Plant 3' to 4' apart. Prune out occasional upright branches, trim for bushiness. Susceptible to fire blight, red spider mite, scale, and aphids.
Herbicides: These are all listed for the genus—Bensulide, Dichlobenil, Trifluralin. EPTC (P. 'Red Elf' and P. 'Tiny Tim').

Remarks. Best used in large areas (except in locations where fire blight is a problem), cascading over a wall. Leaf, weed, and trash removal can be a problem because of thorny branches. Available in 1-gallon cans.

Other Species. P. 'Tiny Tim' (3′ high, compact growth, smaller leaves, almost no thorns, plant 2′ to 3′ apart); P. 'Red Elf' (similar to P. 'Tiny Tim'); P. 'Walderi' (wide-spreading).

Ranunculus repens	**6-10″**
Creeping Buttercup	**Zone 4**

Evergreen herbaceous perennial native to Europe. Buttercup family (Ranunculaceae).

Characteristics. Long, thick runners creep flat on the ground, rooting at nodes. Fast-growing; can be invasive. Three-parted leaves are dark green, glossy, 1-1½″ wide, roundish, toothed, on long leaf stalks. Bright yellow, cup-shaped flowers are ¾″ across, up to 2′ high, in spring.

Culture. Grows well in heavy soils, slightly acid or slightly alkaline. Needs plenty of water. Partial to full shade, will tolerate some sun with abundant water (leaves lighter green in sun). Plant 12″ apart. Requires frequent edge trimming.
Herbicides: Bensulide (listed for genus).

Remarks. Useful in small areas, narrow spaces, as a bulb cover. Leaves are poisonous if eaten and can blister the skin of sensitive people. The variety listed is more readily available than the species.

Varieties. R.r. pleniflorus (R.r. flore-pleno, R. speciosus) small, double flowers on shorter stems (8-10″), sometimes sold as R. repens, available in flats.

Rosmarinus officinalis	**12-24″ x 4-6′**
'Prostratus'	
Dwarf Rosemary (Creeping	
Rosemary, Prostrate Rosemary)	**Zones 8-9**

Evergreen woody shrub native to the Mediterranean area. Mint family (Labiatae).

Characteristics. Spreading, mounding growth with creeping, rooting stems. Slow to start, moderate growth rate after a year or so. Needle-like leaves are dark green, ¾″ long, aromatic when crushed. Flowers are light blue, ¼-½″ long, in winter and spring, sometimes in fall, not showy from a distance but good up close; attractive to bees.

Culture. Grows in most soils, good drainage is important; tolerates poor and rocky soil. Drought-tolerant but can be watered regularly for more lush growth if drainage is provided. Full sun. Belt 1 seashore. Plant 12″

to 24″ apart. Trim lightly for bushiness. Light feeding will produce lush growth (feeding is not essential and can be overdone).
Herbicides: Diphenamid, EPTC.

Remarks. Good for small or large areas, narrow spaces, cascading over a wall, hot dry slopes; also useful in the herb garden. Very deer-resistant. Tips will occasionally freeze in severe winters. Available in flats, pots, and 1-gallon cans.

Varieties. R.o. 'Lockwood de Forest' (R. foresteri, R. lockwoodii) lighter green leaves, flowers deeper blue, occasionally develops upright branches.

Santolina chamaecyparissus	**1½-2′ x 3-4′**
(S. incana nana)	
Gray Santolina (Cypress Lavender-	
Cotton)	**Zones 6-7**

Evergreen woody sub-shrub from southern Europe. Daisy family (Compositae).

Characteristics. Dense mound of foliage with prostrate, creeping stems. Slow to moderate growth rate. Very finely cut leaves are ½-¾″ long, silvery gray, aromatic when crushed. Flowers are yellow, ¾″ across, button-like heads in summer. Stems are brittle.

Culture. Grows best in light soils, tolerates poor and rocky soils, must have good drainage, tolerates well-drained heavy clay. Drought-resistant, tolerates some watering. Full sun; tolerates heat. Belt 1 seashore. Plant 12″ to 24″ apart. Trim yearly after flowering for neatness, bushiness, and to prevent woodiness (best kept at about 12″ height), replace old plants that get woody and die out in the center (more common when untrimmed).

Remarks. Good for hot, dry slopes, cascading over a wall, beach plantings, small areas only (because of short life), narrow spaces; also useful in the herb garden. Available in flats, pots, and 1-gallon cans.

S. virens	**15″ x 3-4′**
Green Santolina (Green	
Lavender-Cotton)	**Zone 7**

Faster-growing, linear leaves are 2″ long, bright green, smooth. Flower heads smaller (½″). Tolerates more water; fire-resistant.

Sarcococca hookeriana humilis	**12-24″ x 8′**
(S. humilis)	
Sweet Box	**Zone 6**

Evergreen woody shrub native to the Himalayas and western China. Boxwood family (Buxaceae).

Characteristics. Spreads by underground runners to form a dense mass of growth. Slow-growing. Leaves are very dark green, waxy, 1-3" long by ½-¾" wide, narrowly oval and pointed, leathery. Small, very fragrant white flowers in early spring (not showy) followed by shiny blue-black berries (not showy).

Culture. Needs a rich, acid soil with plenty of organic matter. Provide plenty of water for best growth. Partial to full shade, will not tolerate heat. Plant 2' apart. Can be sheared for denser growth and to keep low. Subject to scale.

Remarks. Best in cooler parts of the South. Useful in small areas and narrow spaces (when trimmed), particularly near areas where people can enjoy the fragrance; good for deeply shaded spots. Available in 1-gallon cans.

Sasa pygmaea (Pleioblastus pygmaeus, 6-12" Bambusa pygmaea)
Dwarf Bamboo **Zone 7**

Evergreen to semi-evergreen (cold climates) perennial grass from Japan. Grass family (Gramineae).

Characteristics. Low mass of thin, erect stems, spreading by underground runners. Fast-growing; can be invasive. Leaves are light grayish-green, narrow, 6" long, pointed.

Culture. Grows in any soil. Most lush growth is with regular watering; dryness retards growth (which sometimes is desirable). Full sun. Plant 12" to 18" apart. Needs regular feeding for best growth (do not feed if growth needs to be controlled).

Remarks. Useful in small or large areas, narrow spaces, on slopes. Will cover large areas and invade adjacent lawns or asphalt paving if not confined by a concrete or metal barrier 18" deep at the edge of the bed. Available in 1-gallon cans.

Varieties. S.p. 'Variegata' has white leaf edges.

Saxifraga stolonifera (S. sarmentosa) 4"
Strawberry Begonia (Strawberry Geranium) **Zones 7-8**

Evergreen herbaceous perennial from eastern Asia. Saxifrage family (Saxifragaceae).

Characteristics. Dense clumps of foliage send out thin, wiry runners that root and form a new plant at each node (grows like a strawberry), forming a flat mat. Sometimes slow to start, then moderate growth rate. Begonia-like, fuzzy leaves are rounded with scalloped edges, 2-4" across (smaller in bright locations), medium to dark gray-green with prominent white veins above, reddish-purple surface beneath. Flowers are white, delicate, 1", in open, upright spikes to 24" high, spring to summer, showy.

Culture. Grows in many soils, preferably rich, tolerates heavy clay, acid or alkaline soils. Needs plenty of moisture. Partial to full shade (leaves turn yellow and burn in sun). Plant 6" to 12" apart. Trim off old flower spikes for neatness.

Remarks. Best used in small areas, narrow spaces, as a bulb cover, between stepping stones. Tolerates en-

vironmental stress. Available in pots, 1-gallon cans, and sometimes from neighbors. Commonly grown as a house plant.

Sedum
Stonecrop

Evergreen succulent perennials of the Stonecrop family (Crassulaceae).

Characteristics. Trailing or creeping, rooting stems form a low mat of growth. Very fast-growing. Small star-like flowers are borne profusely in many-flowered clusters. All are shallow rooted. See individual species listing for other characteristics.

Culture. The main requirement is good drainage, best growth is in loamy soil, but will do well in sandy, poor, and rocky soils. Drought-tolerant; best with regular watering (can be overwatered, particularly in summer dormant period). Full sun; tolerate heat. Belt 2 seashore. Plant 6" to 12" apart. Will die out in spots if crowded. Can be occasionally clipped lightly; trim off old flower clusters for neatness.
Herbicides: These are all listed for the genus— Bensulide, Diphenamid, EPTC, Trifluralin.

Remarks. Best used in small areas only, narrow spaces, as a bulb cover. Available in flats, pots, occasionally 1-gallon cans. Easily propagated from cuttings (even tiny pieces).

S. acre 2-4"
Goldmoss Stonecrop **Zone 4**

Native to Europe, North Africa, eastern Asia. Leaves ¼" long, light green. Yellow flowers on short stems, late spring. Can become a pest (every tiny leaf will root and form a plant). Several varieties. Use between stepping stones. Can cause dermatitis in sensitive people. Tolerates environmental stress.

S. album 3-6"
White Stonecrop (Worm-Grass) **Zone 4**

Sometimes sold as S. brevifolium. Native to Europe and Siberia. Leaves ¼" to ½" long, bright medium green, with tints of red in winter. White flowers in summer. A few varieties. Use between stepping stones. Belt 1 seashore.
Herbicides: These are listed for this species— DCPA, Diphenamid, EPTC, Simazine, Trifluralin.

S. anglicum 2-4"
English Stonecrop **Zone 4**

Native to western Europe. Leaves ⅛" to ¼" long, dark green. White to pinkish flowers on short stems, spring. Use between stepping stones.

S. confusum 6-12"
Zone 8

Native to Mexico. Branched mounded growth. Leaves 1-1½" long, ½-¾" wide, light yellow-green. Yellow flowers in late spring. Similar to S. amecamecanum and sometimes sold interchangeably. Good for cascading over a wall.

Native Southern Groundcovers

Interest in native plants for landscape use is growing in gardening circles in these times of increased awareness of and concern for our natural environment. Unfortunately, native groundcovers are scarcely mentioned.

The problem in using many of our native plants is their extremely limited availability. However, there are a few nurserymen in the South who keep in stock or can obtain many of the native groundcovers on this list. The others you will have to propagate yourself.

This list is provided as a starting place for those individuals intrepid enough to seek out and experiment with the materials necessary for the "building" of a naturalistic environment.

Adiantum capillus-veneris (Southern Maidenhair Fern)
Ampelopsis arborea (Pepper Vine)
Asarum canadense (Canadian Wild Ginger)
Asarum shuttleworthii (Mottled Wild Ginger)
Asarum virginicum (Virginia Wild Ginger)
Ascyrum hypericoides (St. Andrew's Cross)
Decumaria barbara (Wood-Vamp)
Dichondra repens (Dichondra, Ponyfoot)
Fragaria virginiana (Wild Strawberry)
Gelsemium sempervirens (Carolina Jessamine)
Hypericum frondosum (Golden St. John's-Wort)

Ipomoea pes-caprae (Beach Morning Glory)
Lorinseria areolata (Chain Fern)
Mitchella repens (Partridge Berry)
Myrica pusilla (Dwarf Wax Myrtle)
Onoclea sensibilis (Sensitive Fern)
Oplismenus hirtellus setarius (Basket Grass)
Oxalis violacea (Violet Wood-Sorrel)
Parthenocissus quinquefolia (Virginia Creeper)
Phlox divaricata (Wild Blue Phlox)
Phlox nivalis (Camla Phlox)
Phlox ovata (Mountain Phlox)
Phlox procumbens (Trailing Phlox)
Phlox stolonifera (Creeping Phlox)
Phlox subulata (Moss-Pink)
Phyla incisa (Texas Frog-Fruit)
Polianthes maculosa
Smilax pumila (Sarsaparilla Vine)
Smilax smallii (Green-Brier)
Symphoricarpos orbiculatus (Indian Currant Coralberry)
Vaccinium myrsinites (Evergreen Blueberry)
Verbena bipinnatifida (Dakota Verbena)
Viola lanceolata (Lance-Leaved Violet)
Viola priceana (Confederate Violet)
Viola primulifolia (Primrose Violet)
Viola walteri (Walter Violet)

S. dasyphyllum	**1-2"**
Gray Stonecrop	**Zone 5**

Native to Europe and northern Africa. Dense, almost moss-like mat. Leaves ⅛" long, bluish-gray. Tiny flowers are white to pinkish, early summer. Use only in smallest areas, between stepping stones.

S. lineare (S. sarmentosum)	**6-8"**
Stringy Stonecrop	**Zone 7**

Native to Japan. Chartreuse green leaves, needle-like, ¾-1" long. Yellow flowers, profuse, spring. Good for cascading over a wall. Tolerates heavy clay soil with drainage. Any little piece will take root.

S. rubrotinctum (S. guatemalense)	**6-8"**
Brown Bean Stonecrop (Christmas Cheer)	**Zones 8-9**

Native to Mexico and Guatemala. Sprawling stems. Jelly-bean-shaped leaves, ¾" long, chartreuse green with reddish tints, often some leaves almost entirely red, particularly in winter. Flowers yellow, spring. Good for cascading over a wall. A very colorful groundcover.

S. rupestre	**6"**
	Zone 7

Native to Portugal. Trailing stems. Needle-like leaves, ½" long, bluish- or grayish-green, turning purplish in winter. Pale yellow flowers on 12-15" stems in summer. Good for cascading over a wall.

S. spurium (S. stoloniferum)	**6"**
Two-Row Stonecrop	**Zone 4**

Native to the Caucasus. Evergreen to semi-evergreen (cold climates). Trailing stems forming a tangled mass. Leaves 1" long, wedge-shaped, thick, dark green, occasionally with bronzy tints. Flowers pale pink, ½", summer. Good for cascading over a wall. S.s. 'Dragons Blood' is 3 to 4" high, has bronzy leaves, rose-red flowers.

Senecio cineraria (Cineraria maritima)	**2-2½'**
Dusty Miller (Silver Groundsel)	**Zones 6-7**

Evergreen herbaceous perennial from the Mediterranean area. Daisy family (Compositae).

Characteristics. Sprawling, dense mound, much branched at the base. Fast-growing. Leaves are 6-8" long, white woolly to ashy gray, deeply cut with many round tipped lobes, looking much like an elongated oak leaf. Flowers are yellow, daisy-like, ½" across in compact clusters, summer, scattered at other seasons.

Culture. Needs well-drained, light, alkaline soil; tolerates poor soil. Drought-tolerant; grows well with light watering. Full sun. Belt 1 seashore. Plant 12" to 18" apart. Trim occasionally for bushiness.

Remarks. Several different plants are named Dusty Miller, which causes much confusion. All are whitish and woolly. One commonly grown in California and frequently sold in southern nurseries is Centaurea cineraria (C. candidissima) which has finely divided (not lobed) leaves that do not resemble oak leaves. Flowers are purple (yellow in some forms), thistle-like, borne singly. More erect-growing and not as suitable for use as a groundcover.

Another Dusty Miller is Artemisia stelleriana (also called Beach Wormwood). This plant is best suited to cold northern climates.

Senecio cineraria is best used in small areas, for difficult hot spots, beach plantings. Available in pots and probably 1-gallon cans.

Thymus serphyllum   **1-6"**
Mother-of-Thyme   **Zone 4**

Evergreen semi-woody perennial from Eurasia and northern Africa. Mint family (Labiatae).

Characteristics. Wiry, creeping, rooting stems form a dense, flat mat. Moderate to fast growth. Leaves are dark green, elliptical, ¼-½" long, aromatic when crushed. Small flowers are lavender, in few-flowered heads, summer, moderately showy.

Culture. Needs light, well-drained soil; tolerates poor, rocky, alkaline or acid soil. Requires dry conditions and full sun, tolerates heat. Belt 2 seashore. Plant 6" to 12" apart. Can be mown or trimmed occasionally.

Remarks. Best used only in small areas, narrow spaces, between stepping stones, as a bulb cover, cascading over a wall. Tolerates some traffic and environmental stress. Available in flats and pots.

Varieties. T.s. albus (White Creeping Thyme, 2-4" high, lower and tighter than other varieties, bright green leaves, white flowers in early summer in profusion); T.s. 'Argenteus' (Silver Creeping Thyme, leaves variegated with silver); T.s. 'Aureus' (Gold Creeping Thyme, leaves variegated with yellow); T.s. coccineus (bright red flowers); T.s. lanuginosus (Woolly Thyme, 2-3" high, tiny gray woolly leaves, pinkish flowers sparsely produced, slightly unkempt in winter); T.s. roseus (pink flowers); T.s. 'Vulgaris' (Lemon Thyme, crushed leaves smell like lemon).

Other Species. T. herba-barona (Caraway Thyme) 2" high, dark green leaves that smell like caraway when crushed; tiny purple flowers. T. vulgaris (Common Thyme) is the common garden herb; not as good a groundcover as other thymes.

Trachelospermum (Rhynchospermum)
Star-jasmine

Evergreen woody vines of the Dogbane family (Apocynaceae).

Characteristics. See individual species listings.

Culture. Best growth is in well-drained soils with plenty of organic matter; tolerate sandy or heavy clay soils, slight alkalinity or acidity. Prefer plenty of water but tolerant of a little dryness (except when young). Full sun to partial shade. Belt 1 seashore. Plant 12" to 18" apart. Basically pest-free.
    Herbicides: Bensulide (listed for genus), EPTC.

Remarks. Available in flats, pots, 1-gallon cans. Very common throughout the lower South.

T. jasminoides   **18-24"**
Confederate Jasmine (Chinese
Star-jasmine)   **Zones 8-9**

Native to China. Not a true jasmine. A twining vine forming a mounding mass when used as a groundcover. Slow to start, moderate to fast rate of growth when established. Leaves are dark green (new foliage light green), shiny, oval, pointed, 1" wide by 2-2½" long, leathery, with bronzy tints and occasional bright red leaves in winter. Flowers are pure white, starlike, ¾-1" across with twisted petals, in loose clusters, very fragrant, profuse and showy, late spring, scattered in summer and fall. Best when trimmed for bushiness. Will climb into trees and shrubs, but easily controlled. Good for large areas, small areas when trimmed low, cascading over a wall. T. j. 'Variegatum' has white variegation on leaves, not commonly available.

T. jasminoides pubescens   **12-18"**
Dwarf Confederate Jasmine   **Zones 8-9**

Proper naming of this plant is subject to debate. Commonly sold as T. asiaticum and referred to as Japanese Star-jasmine or Asiatic Jasmine. Commonly available in the lower South. Twining vine forming an interlacing mass of stems as a groundcover; stems root when they touch the ground.

Slow to start, moderate growth rate after a year or two. All plant parts are like T. jasminoides only smaller; leaves are ¾-1½" long, stems are thinner and more wiry, less vigorous as a climber. Flowers are creamy-white with orange center, not as profuse as T. jasminoides. Plants must be several years old to bloom. Much confusion occurs when T. jasminoides is regularly clipped, thus producing leaves the size of T.j. pubescens.

Weeds are a problem for a year or two because of slow growth. Bermuda grass can cause trouble in established plantings. Trim for more compact growth, but not too low or weeds will regenerate. Useful in small or large areas, narrow spaces; not attractive when cascading over a wall (too stringy). Young growth tips are often killed in cold winters, producing a brownish top coat on plantings that have been clipped regularly.

A variegated form has lighter green leaves with whitish variegation; sometimes called White Mist Jasmine.

T. asiaticum   18″
Japanese Star-jasmine (Asiatic
Jasmine, Yellow Star-jasmine)   **Zones 7-8**

Native to Japan and Korea. This name is used in the trade to refer to T. jasminoides pubescens, a common groundcover in the lower South. T. asiaticum is not widely grown. The habit of growth is more like T. jasminoides, although less vigorous (will climb to 15′ eventually with support). Leaves are smaller, broader and not as sharp pointed; new growth is bronzy. Flowers larger, petals wider, creamy yellow, darker yellow in the center, spring. Leaves not as prominently veined on the surface as T.j. pubescens.

Verbena peruviana (V. chamaedrifolia)   4-6″
Peruvian Verbena   **Zones 8-9**

Evergreen herbaceous perennial native to South America. Verbena family (Verbenaceae).

Characteristics. Prostrate, creeping, rooting stems form a flat mat. Very fast-growing. Leaves are medium to dark olive-green, 1-2″ long, narrowly oval, coarsely hairy, toothed. Flowers are vivid red, small, in many flowered, flat clusters, on short erect spikes, profuse in spring through fall.

Culture. Grows in most well-drained soils. Drought-tolerant. Full sun, tolerates heat. Plant 12″ to 18″ apart. Weeds may be a problem as growth is not dense, replanting occasionally necessary as old plants thin out in the middle. Susceptible to red spider mite, mildew.

Remarks. Best for small areas only, narrow spaces, difficult hot spots. Not a long-lived solution but good for a quick short term cover. Available in flats, possibly pots.

Varieties. These are slower-growing and taller: V.p. 'Appleblossom' (8-12″, soft pink); V.p. 'Little Pinkie' (rose pink); V.p. 'Princess Gloria' (salmon); V.p. 'Raspberry Rose' (rose, 10-15″).

Vinca
Periwinkle

Evergreen perennial vines native to Europe and Asia. Dogbane family (Apocynaceae).

V. major   18-24″
Bigleaf Periwinkle (Common-
Periwinkle)   **Zones 7-8**

Characteristics. Long, trailing, rooting stems interlace to build up mounds of growth. Moderate growth rate. Dark green leaves are oval, glossy, 2″ long. Flowers are bright blue to lavender-blue, funnel-shaped, 1-2″ across, scattered, spring and summer.

Culture. Grows in almost any soil, best with plenty organic matter. Needs plenty of water. Full sun with plenty of water (cool climates), partial shade (hot climates), will tolerate heat if in the shade. Belt 3 seashore. Plant 12″ to 24″ apart. Trim occasionally for bushiness, until established. Fertilize for best growth.
Herbicides: Bensulide (listed for genus), Diphenamid, EPTC, Trifluralin.

Remarks. Best for large areas, shady slopes, cascading over a wall. Deer-resistant, tolerates environmental stress and root competition of trees. Available in flats, pots, 1-gallon cans.

Varieties. V.m. variegata (creamy white leaf variegation); V.m. aurea variegata (gold leaf variegation).

V. minor   6″
Dwarf Periwinkle (Creeping Myrtle)   **Zone 5**

Characteristics. Trailing, rooting stems, sometimes mounding, forming a dense mat. Moderate growth rate. Leaves like those of V. major only smaller (¾-1½″ long). Lavender-blue, 1″ flowers, scattered, early spring and again in fall.

Culture. Prefers rich soil with plenty of organic matter, tolerates others except poor soils. Needs plenty of water regularly. Partial to full shade. Plant 12″ to 18″ apart. Requires more care than V. major (more water and regular feeding), trim yearly for more even, compact growth.
Herbicides: Bensulide (listed for genus), DCPA, Diphenamid, EPTC, Trifluralin (possible slight injury). *Not recommended:* Dichlobenil, Simazine.

Remarks. Good for small or large areas, narrow spaces, bulb cover, cascading over a wall, shady slopes. Best in cooler parts of the South. Deer-resistant, tolerates environmental stress. Available in flats, pots, 1-gallon cans.

Varieties. V.m. 'Alba' (white flowers); V.m. 'Atropurpurea' (purple flowers); V.m. 'Bowles Variety' (grows as a clump, non-running, light blue flowers); V.m. 'Multiplex' (double purple flowers); V.m. 'Variegata' (blue flowers, yellow leaf variegation).

Viola odorata   8″
Sweet Violet   **Zones 6-7**

Evergreen herbaceous perennial from Europe, Asia, Africa. Violet family (Violaceae).

Characteristics. Tufted clump of foliage sending out long runners that root and form plants at nodes. Moderate to fast growth rate. Heart-shaped leaves are dark green, 2-4″, round-toothed. Small flowers are dark violet, fragrant, not showy from a distance but pleasant up close, spring.

Culture. Grows in many well-drained soils, acid or alkaline; best in rich soil with plenty organic matter. Needs regular watering. Partial to full shade. Plant 12″ apart. Blooms best if fertilized in early spring prior to blooming.

Remarks. Use in small areas, narrow spaces, as a bulb cover, in the woodland garden. Available in pots and probably 1-gallon cans.

Varieties and Other Species. The horticultural varieties available are numerous, with flower colors of deep violet, bluish-violet, rose, and white, some double-flowered. There are also many species native to the South growing under a variety of conditions (availability of these is limited).

V. hederacea	3″ x 10-12″
Australian Violet	**Zones 8-9**

Spreads by rooting runners, bright green heart-shaped leaves, light blue and silver flowers, spring and summer.

Wedelia trilobata	12-18″
Wedelia	**Zones 9-10**

Evergreen (tender) herbaceous perennial from tropical America. Daisy family (Compositae)

Characteristics. Thick, creeping, rooting runners interlace to form lush, dense mounds of growth. Very fast-growing; can be invasive. Leaves are medium to dark green with three pointed lobes, 2″ long, coarsely hairy. Golden-yellow, daisy-like flowers, 1″ across, showy most of the year.

Culture. Grows in most soils, well-drained or wet (not boggy). Tolerates some dryness, best with plenty of water. Full sun to partial shade (flowers best in sun). Belt 2 seashore. Plant 18″ apart. Requires frequent edge trimming and trimming against vertical surfaces (walls, fences) where it mounds up, can be sheared to keep under control.

Remarks. Any frost kills the tops which re-grow in spring if ground does not freeze. Useful in large areas (zone 10) or small areas if trimmed, good for cascading over a wall. Commonly used in Florida; not readily found in most other areas. Available in pots, possibly 1-gallon cans. Easily grown from cuttings.

Zoysia tenuifolia	3-6″
Korean Grass (Mascarene Grass,	
Velvet Grass)	**Zone 8**

Perennial grass from the Mascarene Islands. Grass family (Gramineae).

Characteristics. Very fine-textured stoloniferous grass, forming a dense bumpy mat when mature. Slow-growing. Leaves are wire-like, light to medium yellow-green, turning straw-colored with frost (retains some of the green in mild climates).

Culture. Grows in most well-drained soils, slightly acid is best, tolerates slight alkalinity. Tolerates some dryness; best with plenty of water. Full sun to partial shade (too much shade causes thin growth). Plant 2″ square plugs 6″ to 12″ apart. Mowing is not necessary (more interesting as a groundcover with its natural hummocky appearance when unmowed). White grub, brown patch, and rust are potential problems although not serious.

Herbicides: See table on page 58 for recommendations. Weeds can be a problem because of slow growth.

Remarks. Useful in small or large areas, narrow spaces, between stepping stones. Tolerates traffic which keeps it flat. Available in flats.

Index

Southern Groundcovers